practical CLASSICS
& CAR RESTORER

Scimitar Restoration

Published by

KELSEY PUBLISHING

Printed in Singapore by
Stamford Press Pte Ltd,
209 Kallang Bahru, Singapore 339344,
for Kelsey Publishing Ltd, Kelsey House,
High Street, Beckenham, Kent BR3 1AN
on behalf of EMAP National
Publications Ltd

ISBN 1 873098 20 0

Acknowledgements

On the mechanical work we would
particularly like to thank Eric
Gilbert who did the bulk of the work
and also Ted Landon who undertook
the servo overhaul plus Miles Wilkins
who provided the expertise on glass
fibre and John Williams who did the
majority of the editorial coverage.

Contents

Introduction

This book is based on the original Reliant Scimitar Restoration 'mini' book, which has been uprated (improved in quality) and had a further 30 pages added. All coverage is compiled from articles which originally appeared in *Practical Classics & Car Restorer*.

All the mechanical work was done on the Practical Classics 'staff car' Scimitar, which had been thoroughly well used (at an average of 30,000 miles a year). The work was carried out by Eric Gilbert and Ted Landon, with the magazine coverage undertaken by John Williams (the then editor).

The Scimitar v Stag feature is a fascinating 'head to head' comparison between two cars which were both very similar in appeal but, completely different in concept. The subject of glass fibre was expertly covered by Miles Wilkins (the famous Lotus specialist) and is an invaluable guide to the subject. The whole book probably now represents the most comprehensive DIY guide to the Scimitar available anywhere. We are sure that owners and enthusiasts will find it useful and interesting.

*Hi there!
Not disturbing you am I?*

Paul Ski

T hink back to the seventies and the relative multiplicity of sporting cars on the market and two will stand apart from the rest – not because they were necessarily *better* than their contemporaries but because they were *different*. Yes, the Triumph Stag and the Reliant Scimitar were each in their way unique — sporting cars yet not sports cars, four-seaters but not saloons. They both had style, large engines by British standards and that hard to define aura of 'class' — arrive anywhere in the Stag or a Scimitar and you'd be seen to be different, out of the rut and very definitely a few notches above those with mere sports cars like the MGB, Triumph GT6 or TR. Racing drivers, royalty, film stars and managing directors of substantial com-

panies were at times to be seen in them, which served even more to enhance the image and flatter the more ordinary owner.

While similar in concept the two cars were very different in specification; and there were contradictions too. One was made by a large manufacturer — Triumph — yet was powered not by a normal production engine but by an exotic, twin overhead camshaft V8 unique to itself. The other, the product of a small specialist assembler, used a very ordinary mass-production power unit — and much in addition that was off someone else's shelf. Then viewed commercially, the car that achieved the greatest production totals was adjudged the failure, while that with the

The Triumph Stag promised much but delivered it falteringly. Graceful Michelotti styling, soft top and a unique power unit combine to make an exclusive grand tourer. Rear view is as neat as the front and the disappearing hood is a superbly executed detail.

lesser figure a success, because in exercising such judgement, expectations and scale must be taken into account — and Triumph, surely, expected to build far more than the 25,877 Stags than did actually leave Speke and Coventry, while Reliant were pleasantly surprised with the GTE's reception and were no doubt proud of the 14,715 that were issued from Tamworth.

The shapes of both cars were inspired by outside concerns — in the case of the Stag, from a styling exercise on a Triumph 2000 saloon by Michelotti, while in the case of the GTE, a British styling house, Ogle. In looks both cars were attractive, the Triumph in a

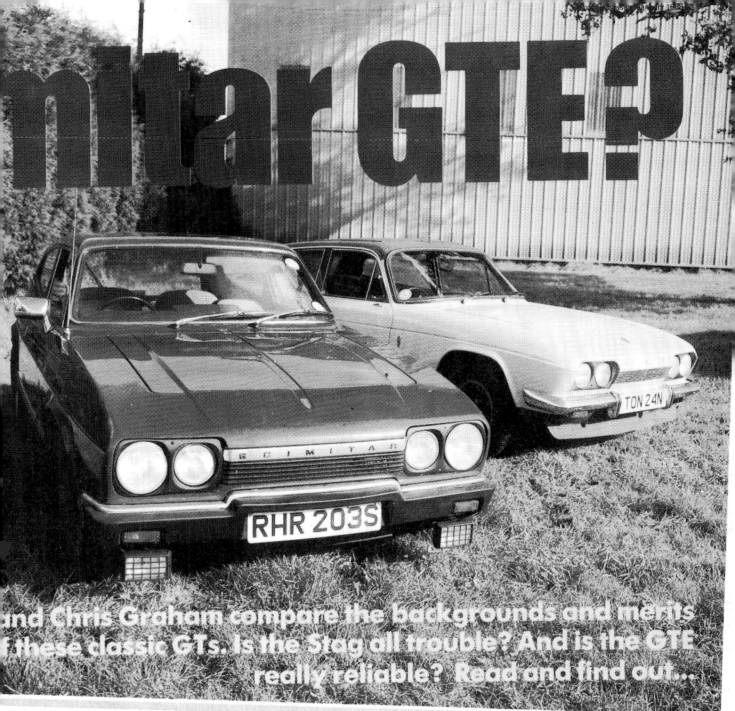

...milar GTE?

...nd Chris Graham compare the backgrounds and merits f these classic GTs. Is the Stag all trouble? And is the GTE really reliable? Read and find out...

more lithe, Italian way and the Reliant in a confident, beefy British manner; but it was the GTE that was perhaps the more significant, setting — or at least anticipating — the trend towards sporting hatchbacks that would, by the early 1980s, predominate over the traditional three-box saloon (though one mustn't forget the true pioneering role of the A40 Farina in this respect; the hatchback Austin emerged in 1958).

In looks and in components such as the suspension and drive train the Stag was related to the Triumph 2000 saloon of 1963, but otherwise shared surprisingly little with its closed long wheelbase cousin — no common body pressings, for example, which

must have raised the unit cost of the car considerably. It arrived (perhaps rather too soon despite a protracted development period) in June 1970 accompanied by an advertising campaign which more than hinted that Triumph intended the new car to challenge such as Mercedes and Alfa Romeo.

I did a fair mileage in RVC 435H (*Motor's* road test Stag of the period) and liked it. It was at its best over long distances, when it would lope along without effort at 90mph and indicated 120mph given reasonable conditions. I don't now recall the wind noise which

was criticised in the September 1970 road test; just the smooth, easy progress of the car, a virtue endowed by its all-independent suspension and power steering as much as by the V8 engine.

As an XK120 owner I naturally didn't rate it a sports car but I was considerably taken with it as a rapid and comfortable Grand Tourer. We didn't know anything about the engine's fragility then and I thought the car marred in only one important respect — the famous 'twitch' which would occur after

The unmistakable outline of the Scimitar GTE, born 1968 yet still handsome — and practical — today. This (right) is the wider, roomier SE6 produced from 1976 (SE6a top, foreground).

The GTE purist's choice? The SE5a (top, background) is considered by many to have the best performance/handling combination of any Scimitar.

Immediate forebear of the GTE was the Scimitar coupe, also glassfibre bodied but with a conventional roofline; a very pretty car in its own right.

The Stag's 145bhp 2,994cc V8 engine was both its glory and its downfall; further development from where Triumph left off has cured many of its inherent faults but rumours of unreliability dealt the car a death-blow in the seventies.

The Stag in 'Mk 1' form; this early car has no coachlines but does have light grey grille and rear wing badges. If the hood had been up the rear quarterlight panels, omitted on Mk 2 cars, could have been seen.

Another contemporary photograph, this showing the later Mk 1 Stag, now adorned by side stripes, black badging and black sills. These cars had Rostyle type hubcaps, which preceded the alloy or optional wire wheels of Mk 2 variants.

accelerating hard round a corner or even after a burst of acceleration on the straight. We attributed it to drive-shaft spline lock-up releasing itself, aided by wind-up in the trailing arm bushes; now it can be eradicated —

Triumph never bothered to and at the time I found it annoying enough not to have bought a Stag had I been in the position of being able to. A pity; its actual handling was responsive yet progressive and its grip high.

The Stag lasted seven years exactly, leaving production in June 1977. Around February 1973 a Mk II version arrived, this having matt black sills and tail panel, double coachline, new wheel trims and revisions to the interior which included new instruments and a smaller diameter steering wheel. Hard and soft tops were standardised while, on the mechanical side, overdrive had been standardised in October the previous year (you could of course still specify the Borg-Warner Model 35 box instead) and the engine's compression ratio upped from 8.8:1 to 9.25:1 in line with the Dolomite which used half its engine in Sprint form.

Thereafter the car received minimal attention — or investment — from Triumph with mainly cosmetic alterations only being featured, although alloy wheels replaced the wire wheel option in April 1973. October 1975 saw brushed aluminium sill covers, the alloy wheels standardised and the rear panel finished in body colours. Other than that, body, engine and suspension were more or less left alone, twitch and all.

By the time the Stag arrived in 1970 the Scimitar GTE had been around for approaching two years, having been launched in October 1968 as the SE5. You might have surmised that underneath its radical new body lay a development of the Scimitar coupé chassis frame but in fact this was all-new with a wheelbase that was 8in greater.

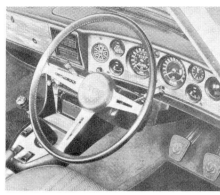

Brochure shot of the Mk 1 interior, illustrating the larger steering wheel and different instrumentation.

Suspension followed coupé practice however, with TR6 wishbone front suspension and a well-located live rear axle. At 14ft 3in, the GTE was 2¾in shorter than the Triumph Stag but an inch wider; it looked the bulkier car though in fact was (at 21½cwt) a lot lighter than the 26cwt Stag. It was slightly cheaper too — the basic 1970 Stag was £2,222, the Scimitar £2,146, though overdrive was standard on the Triumph and an extra on the Reliant.

The GTE went through various changes up until 1980, when volume production ceased; the original SE5 had been powered by the Mk IV Zodiac version of the 3-litre Ford V6 engine but on the arrival of the SE5a in 1972 its place was taken by the Granada-spec. unit. Likewise the Mk IV Zodiac gearbox was phased out in 1973, replaced by an amalgam of Transit casing and 3-litre Capri

On the road the Stag was effortless and elegant with good road manners only blemished by what's been termed the 'seven year twitch', the wind-up in the rear suspension that Triumph never did sort out during the car's production life.

An indirect ancestor of the GTE ('Grand Touring Estate') was the remarkable GTS ('Glazing Test Special') produced by Ogle and Triplex in 1966; the Duke of Edinburgh owned the car for some 18 months which considerably boosted Reliant's image as a constructor.

The GTE's rear hatch wasn't unique (Jaguar's fixed-head 'E'-type of 1961 had a similar arrangement) but the semi-estate styling provided a generous amount of luggage room for a sporting two-plus-two, as owner Mike Wollacott demonstrates.

The term 'yuppie' hadn't been invented but, if it had, that's who Triumph were aiming the Stag at. The mood is well evoked by this brochure page of a late Mk 2 car.

Mechanical specifications

	Triumph Stag	Reliant Scimitar SE5/5a	SE6b
Capacity	2,997cc	2,994cc	2,792cc
Configuration	8-cyl, 90 deg 'V'	6-cyl, 60 deg 'V'	
Cams	Overhead, one per bank	Single, in block	
Bore/stroke	86 x 64.5	93.67 x 72.42	93.02 x 68.50
Carburettors	2 x Zenith Stromberg	Weber 40 DFA1	Solex-Pierburg downdraught twin choke
BHP at RPM	145 at 5,500	138 at 5,000	135 at 5,200
Transmission	4-speed + overdrive Borg-Warner Type 35	4-speed manual, O/D, automatic	3-speed auto
Suspension	F — MacPherson strut R — semi-trailing arm	F — Ind. coil, and wishbones. R — trailing arms, Watts linkage	F — Ind. coil double wishbones. R — trailing arms, Watts linkage

Facts and figures

	Triumph Stag	Reliant Scimitar SE5/5a	SE6b
Wheelbase	100in	99in	103.8in
Length	173.75in	170in	174.5in
Height	49.5in	52.5in	52in
Weight (cwt)	25	22.7(A) 22.7(OD) 21.8(M)	24.3(A)
Tyre size (ins)	155 x 13	185 x 14	185 x 14
Rim size	5.5in	5in J	6in (5.5in steel wheel)
0-60mph	9.7 secs (M)	12.8 secs	11.7 secs
50-70mph in top	7.7(M)	10.1(M)	7.1(A)
Overall mpg	20	20.4	20.5

internals — plus the advantage of the very good J-type overdrive which was then an option on the Transit.

Next big change for the car was its metamorphosis into the SE6 — described by at least one Scimitar pundit as "an undeveloped disaster!". Mechanically similar to the SE5a, the new model boasted a larger, roomier body mounted on a revised chassis and, announced at the 1976 Motor Show, it was intended to appeal more to the 'executive' market. It didn't, at least, not very much, perhaps because at £5,288 the 'executive' could avail himself instead of such as a BMW 320i (and save £50 into the bargain, although it was still cheaper than the Stag at £5,854). Against such competition Reliant gradually found it harder to sell GTEs, especially as some of the car's appeal to the sporting set had been lost due to over-soft suspension settings — though this point at least was soon rectified with the advent of the SE6a which sold much better.

The last big change for the Scimitar was the adoption of the 2.8 'Cologne' engine in 1979, the car being tagged then as the SE6b,

though a new model, the GTC convertible, came in 1980; but the GTC simply didn't sell, Reliant being left with rows of unsold cars outside their factory. GTE and GTC production ended once and for all in November 1986, though from 1981 the build rate had been hardly more than a trickle.

Driving a Scimitar GTE is altogether different from conducting a Stag; I loved them when they were new and now, re-acquainted with the type some 14 years on, the appeal remains — the car doesn't have the delicate touch of the Stag and the ride is more wooden, but there's a tough, no-nonsense feel to it and — SE6 apart — cornering is very neutral with a responsive turn-in. I recall that the Scimitar coupe prior to 1968 was a slightly tail-happy beast in the wet but this doesn't seem the case with the GTE, at least on today's tyres. And with that immensely

useful tail-gate, the GTE remains an enjoyable long-distance tourer, unsubtle perhaps but with a practicality that outweighs the lack of an open top.

Which to buy — Stag or Scimitar? I wouldn't presume to chose for you as both cars have their own merits which appeal to different people; but even though the Scimitar is hardly bug-free (as you'll read in our 'Buying for restoration' section), the odds are that it'll provide more miles per hassle than the Stag and if you don't take satisfaction from weekend fettling, then it's the Reliant for you. But then, if you want the same sort of pace with more grace — plus the bonus of open air motoring — you can hardly ignore the Stag. Whatever — both these cars have immense *character* and you won't have a dull moment with either! ☐

Paul Skilleter

The parts scene

Stag — growing values and co-operative ventures paint a bright picture.

The Triumph Stag is now going through that change of status which, with luck, is the lot of most worthwhile older cars. Simply, values are rising on the open market to the extent that it is making a little more sense to spend money on reviving tired Stags — which, in turn, produces more rebuilt and therefore more valuable Stags which further encourages a rise in prices. The Stag is now firmly locked-in to this self-fuelling system of spiralling values with the result that the re-manufacture of NLS ('no longer stocked') BL parts by specialists is now increasingly under way.

While some might mourn the passing of the 'cheap Stag', ultimately the system works to the benefit of both car and owner, as the latter finds it easier to renovate poor examples which might otherwise be broken and so contributes to the car's survival rate; this bodes well for future generations of Stag enthusiasts and for the continuance of spare parts re-manufacture.

Overall the parts situation for Stags is good in that there's nothing which can't be obtained which would keep a car off the road. A reducing number of spares is carried by BL still, currently including front wings and sills (both normally stocked by Stag specialists). Fitting complete front wings is not always necessary though as most rusted areas in this region are more easily dealt with using widely available repair sections. Front valances are available from specialists, these being produced on ex-BL tooling.

On the minus side, original rear wings and bootlids are nearly impossible to find and some 'pattern' rear wings on the market "require fitting" as the time-honoured phrase goes — which is another way of saying that you might find them an inch too long (or maybe short!). In any case they are huge panels, nearly six feet in length. The situation will be eased when, by the new year, remanufactured bootlids will be in the hands of specialists, with the expectation that 1988 will also see more acceptable rear wings appear (meanwhile, repair panels cope with most of the normal wheel-arch trouble

GTE — mass-production parts and good specialist back-up aid owners.

With the GTE technically still available as a new car up to a year ago, it's in a different category altogether from the Stag whose production ended very definitely in 1977.

Reliant themselves, however, now have little to do with the GTE — having moved on to the SS1 — and the parts operation for the newer cars has been contracted out to Unipart since February 1987. But as it is unlikely that High Street Unipart outlets carry much for the Scimitar in stock it is once again the specialists to whom the owner usually turns.

As you would expect, those components which originally emanated from Ford (engine/drive train) or Triumph (front suspension) are obtainable off-the-shelf. The situation with those items produced solely for the GTE is patchy, especially as Unipart discarded a lot of the inventory which showed little movement (but which may have been vital to restorers). Original trim and brightwork for the SE5 is, for example, very scarce and that for the SE6 is going the same way. However, with GTE prices just about turning the corner, the re-manufacturing

High underbonnet temperatures appear to affect the Ford V6 engine but at least spares are no problem. A complete overhaul means removing the unit of course, but heads can be overhauled and pistons removed for a mid-term revival with the block in situ.

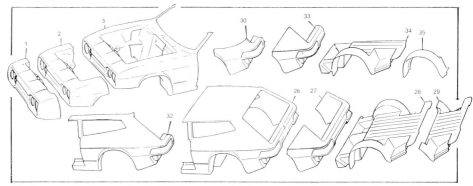

Replacement body parts for the GTE are available in a number of different sections as this extract from Graham Walker's catalogue shows.

The TR-type trunnion used on the Scimitar can wear rapidly, either internally or where the wishbone pivot locates as here. A trunnion costs around £20, a bush kit £8; if the vertical link's threads have worn as a consequence, that costs about £20 to replace.

process is getting under way.

To start with basics, brand-new chassis frames are listed for around the £1,000 mark but are rarely needed — more often required are outriggers and brackets costing from £6, which is more like it! As for bodyshells, these were originally two huge mouldings, the floorpan and the outer top body; technically they too are available but in reality only 'cor-

ners' or specific sections are ever needed unless you've contrived to roll the car. These sections are available in great variety for the SE6, less for the SE5. If anything they are dearer than their steel equivalents — but then, they are normally only required to make good accident damage as Scimitars don't suffer the curse of rust.

Trim and brightware are difficult areas

spots). One continuing problem for those involved in the ground-up restoration of a really poor Stag has been the absence of passenger compartment and boot floors which, in fact, were never available as 'official' spare parts; however, the good news is that these too are in the pipeline and will shortly be available — if they aren't already.

On the mechanical side everything normally needed for the maintenance and overhaul of the V8 engine is obtainable and one specialist made the point to us that since the engine's specification was drawn up, materials and quality-control for component manufacture have considerably improved, pistons, piston rings and bearings all being examples. In addition today's rebuilt engines can be further improved over the original by the fitting of modified or uprated components such as stronger cylinder head studs — in EN19 steel and these are said to increase head and gasket life "dramatically". A duplex camshaft chain set is on the cards for 1988 too. Incidentally there has been controversy about bearing failure caused by oil filter faults cutting off the supply of lubricant to the V8's crankshaft; the best advice seems to be to fit the correct Unipart filter so that at least you'll have a valid warranty claim!

All suspension bushes and joints can be found 'off the shelf', though the Stag's independent rear end contains a lot of them so a suspension overhaul isn't cheap. If you are contemplating such a job, however, the Stag's characteristic rear-end 'twitch' can now be eradicated by fitting stiffer rear suspension bushes which are immune to the wind-up suffered by the standard variety. Good quality, gas-filled dampers are another worthwhile improvement on 'OE' equipment and will further enhance the Stag's already excellent handling and ride qualities.

In respect of trim and interior parts the Stag owner is probably better-off than his Scimitar counterpart, as there were fewer changes and fewer difficult-to-reproduce one-off mouldings used in the Triumph. It can be anticipated that, as time goes on, those items which aren't currently available will be within a very few years. Secondhand parts can sometimes be found to fill the gap but, as fewer cars are now broken, this source will diminish. The number of surviving cars is not immense but there are enough to make reproduction viable and it is pleasant to record that generally speaking, Stag specialists co-operate among themselves so that duplication is avoided and the greatest possible number of 'missing' parts re-appear in their stock-lists each year. □

Spare parts — typical prices

	Triumph Stag	Reliant Scimitar
Front wing	£60	£250
Rear wing	£150 (pattern)	—
	£60 (glass fibre)	
Wheel arch repair section (outer F or R)	£30	—
Door	£175	£60
Bonnet	£95 (new)	£84
Bootlid	£135 (new)	£20 (SE4)
Exhaust	£130 (s/steel)	£135 (s/steel)
Steering rack	£75 exch (recon.)	£55-£130 exch
Halfshaft	£75 exch (recon.)	—
Shock absorber	£50pr (gas adj.)	£30-£60
Spring	£15	£16
Brake master cyl	£60 (new)	£50-£100
Clutch	£60	£82
Clutch master cyl	£30	£46-£58
Road wheels	£40 (alloy, new)	£20 (chrome/alloy)
	£15 (steel, new)	£10 (steel)
Oil pump	£30	£25-£40
Carburettor	£30pr (exch, s.hand)	—
Distributor	£90 (new)	£7 — cap
Hardtop	£75-£200	—
Hood	£75-£250 exch	—

Restoration jobs — typical prices compared

	Triumph Stag	Reliant Scimitar
Engine rebuild	£1,000-1,500	£500-600
Front susp rebuild	£300-400 (top bushes not available)	£200-400
Front wing repl.	£250-400	£800-1,200
Full service	£95-120	£80-90
(All prices quoted are subject to VAT).		

Vacuum moulded dash and console on later GTEs tends to crack but non-original lookalike GRP replacements are now coming onto the market. They're a bit awkward to fit (GRP doesn't bend like moulded plastic) but once in are a permanent answer to the problem.

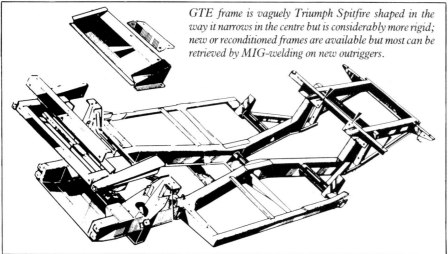

GTE frame is vaguely Triumph Spitfire shaped in the way it narrows in the centre but is considerably more rigid; new or reconditioned frames are available but most can be retrieved by MIG-welding on new outriggers.

and the SE5 restorer must constantly be on the look-out for 'finds' at autojumbles or among fellow club members if he is rebuilding to strictly original specification. Cars are still being broken quite regularly though and numbers of specialists still sell second-hand items. However, seats, steering wheels, facia panels and fixed quarter-lights (the pivoted originals are very scarce) are examples of recent re-manufacture and this is indicative of a growing trend. As with the Stag specialists, Scimitar specialists often get together and each will choose to reproduce one particular item, thus avoiding unnecessary duplication and increasing the range of newly-available parts. To sum up the GTE spares situation one could therefore say that it is quite good but — so far as the SE5 range is concerned — bound to improve with time.

Bodywork
— Stag

The Triumph Stag is a popular target for thieves. This example was stolen and stripped and is seen here in the as-found condition.

The condition of a Stag's bodywork takes a very definite second place to the engine with regard to importance although it is still sensible to be alert since work in this area also can be expensive. The Stag fares better than most with regard to corrosion but, when it does go, it is in all the usual places such as the front and rear wheel arches, the sills (particularly

There are several characteristic areas where rust occurs on the Stag and the front wheel arch is one of them. The spot welding and the close proximity of the panels make rust a certainty here.

expensive to repair), the door bottoms, the boot lid, the rear panel and the edges of the hardtop. It is also likely that you will find a very damp boot compartment so lift the carpets and check the floor area carefully. This applies to the passenger compartment as well.

Fortunately, a reasonably wide selection of repair sections and original panels is available and so most jobs are possible.

— Scimitar

For sheer durability glass fibre bodywork is ininitely superior to steel, but that doesn't mean to say that you can blithely ignore bodywork condition when purchasing a Scimitar. This is because repairs to GRP bodies are often difficult and call for the acquisition of specialist skills, particularly when it comes to tackling gel-coat cracks and local repairs. Yes, anyone can cut out a damaged section and stick in a new piece, but preventing the work from showing once the paint's on is a different matter altogether!

Pay careful attention to the condition of the GTE's body therefore, in respect of stress cracking and badly-repaired damage. Buy the best-looking car you can find for your money, placing body condition over mechanical condition in importance. Restoring a poor Scimitar body is difficult and, if you pay someone to do it, very expensive — it could actually cost more than to eradicate an average amount of rust in a goodish Stag body . . .

Drive train
— Stag

With regard to the Stag transmission it can be said that, in general terms, there are few problems to be encountered but those that are will inevitably be expensive. The manual box can suffer from worn synchromesh and the overdrive, if fitted, can sometimes have become sluggish in operation. The automatic box can develop harsh change and kick-down problems and for checking this refer to our comments regarding the Scimitar. If the clutch on a car seems worn it is worth remembering that it will take a skilled mechanic a whole day to change it and should this be required it will be expensive. If you plan to do it yourself it might be wise to allow a weekend to make the swap.

— Scimitar

The Scimitar used variously the Mk IV Zodiac Z-type gearbox or the Granada S-type and the vast majority of GTEs came with overdrive. The correct functioning or otherwise of the gearbox should be obvious on driving the car, the same applying to the overdrive. Reconditioned units are available for relatively modest sums so that a poor gearbox or malfunctioning overdrive does not represent a terminal situation — except that parts for the early (Zodiac) boxes are no longer plentiful. If you are looking at an automatic car, test the gearbox by ensuring that the gear changes are virtually instantaneous and that the kick-down facility is reasonably responsive.

The rear axles are more of concern with a Scimitar as they are prone to failure due to contamination of the differential oil through the condensation which occurs when the axle cools after a run. This can result in pitting and rusting of the gears and bearings and to prevent it regular oil changes are needed — say at least once a year. Such attention will also reveal loss of oil from the front oil seals, an equally common occurrence which can also lead to failure. A correctly reconditioned rear axle with new gears can cost £350, so listen for a 'rumbly' rear axle on your test drive. The Salisbury axle assembly is unique to the Scimitar even if the actual differential is shared with such as Jaguar and Aston Martin.

The good news is that you haven't a steel structure underneath the outer panels to fester away; rot can occur in chassis outriggers and bracketry, so these should be inspected, but even then local repairs can be effected without having to remove the body — which is a feasible proposition but only if you're intent on a full, last-nut-and-bolt restoration.

Suspension/ steering
— Scimitar

The front suspension of the Scimitar is Triumph TR and presents a weak point on the car — it's essential that the threaded trunnions are very regularly greased other-

TR6-type front suspension is used on the GTE; top ball joint is long-lasting but the bottom trunnion needs greasing every thousand miles to prevent premature wear.

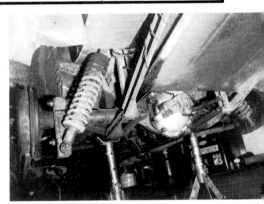

Rear axle with its attachment points for coil spring/damper units and Watts linkage is unique to the Scimitar; also visible are parts of the chassis frame, including the rust-prone body brackets.

wise water gets in and extensive wear quickly develops. Sometimes you can detect that this has happened from stiff steering, but not always, and it may be as well mentally to budget for trunnion replacement just in case.

GTE steering employs a LHD Austin 1800 rack mounted upside down; power steering was standardised from January 1981 and was an optional extra prior to that on the SE6 — worthwhile too, because steering effort otherwise is quite high. Exchange or new racks and PAS pumps are available.

— Stag

The suspension system of MacPherson struts at the front and semi-trailing arms at the rear is, on the face of it, a robust system which serves the Stag well. However, the problems that do occur come as a result of perished and worn rubber bushes. A replacement set of rubber bushes, although being rather expensive to have fitted (upwards of £500), can make a surprising difference to the feel of the whole car and greatly improve its road manners. □

Engine

— Scimitar

The Ford V6 Essex was built in huge numbers but, even so, it possessed a number of inherent faults, some of which seemed to be aggravated by its installation in the Scimitar — perhaps due to the heat-retaining glassfibre 'cocoon' around it. Very regular oil changes are considered essential, failing which the engine can become very 'tired' at a quite low mileage, so take a look at the dipstick and judge whether the owner has neglected this chore.

With the cooling system in perfect condition the engine doesn't run hot but a slight deficiency somewhere will bring trouble — particularly as the engine is prone to pushing out a lot of water expansion, a loss which, if not noticed, can lead to problems such as head gasket failure. In fact gasket failure is an important clue to a neglected or abused engine so check inside the oil filler cap for light-coloured gunge and check the water for traces of oil. If the owner says the head gaskets were recently renewed it won't necessarily mean all is now well — the experts say that it's crucial to obtain clinically clean mating surfaces and to use a Ford gasket with no 'goo' when re-seating the aluminium heads, otherwise you might as well not have bothered.

Cam drive wheel and oil pump drive shaft failures aren't unknown with the V6 and, if you're looking at an early Scimitar, note that the plain Tufnell type cam drive gear was changed to cast iron with nylon teeth in 1971 — the year when the engine was given 'D' shaped inlet ports found by Weslake to be more efficient than the previous oval ones; a larger oil pump was fitted to engines after that too. It's worth noting that all post-1968 V6 blocks will accept this and other later hardware if you want to update during an overhaul. Spares for all but the pre-1968 V6 engines are plentiful and more reasonably priced than for the Stag power unit and rebuild costs are dramatically lower — at least half, with the added advantage that it's more of a DIY unit than the specialised Stag one. Needless to say this applies to the late 2.8 litre engines too.

— Stag

If you are considering a Triumph Stag as your next classic steed your pre-purchase inspection should most definitely begin with the engine. It is the single most important area when evaluating a Stag and, if you are not sure exactly what to look for, our advice is to call on the help of someone who is.

Major problems are common and are always very expensive to rectify. Everyone must have heard tales about cylinder head corrosion associated with this unit and it should be emphasised here that this *is* a real problem. The aluminium heads are bolted (in a complex manner) on to a steel block and once the gaskets become worn (usually after about 20,000 miles) urgent treatment is required. The 'blowing' gasket promotes corrosion which, if left unresolved, can effectively bond the head and block together. Assuming that this situation is caught in time the fitting of replacement gaskets will cost about £200. If not, the bill could be anything up to £1,000

The 3-litre Ford V6 used by all GTEs up to 1979, when the 2.8-litre (still on carburettors) replaced it. Head gasket failure is evidence of poor health and cleanliness of mating surfaces is essential when fitting a replacement.

The Stag engine shared a 'V' configuration with that of the Scimitar but little else, having two extra cylinders and considerably more sophistication.

as special equipment and expertise will be needed.

The water galleries are also prone to corrosion and, where this has occurred badly, a new head is the only alternative. New heads (there are still a few left) cost £600-£800 for a pair and, assuming that the head and block are not completely corroded together, a competent mechanic should be able to make the change within a day. It should be added here that such troubles arise only if the warning signs are ignored in the early stages.

The crankshaft in this engine is a weak component and causes problems. The tiny bearing surfaces on the shaft (they are even smaller than those on a Mini crank!) are barely adequate for the job and wear is very common. Regular oil changes (every 3,000 miles) are probably the best way of putting off the evil day as they lessen the risk of damage from particles of dirt carried in aged oil. Regrinding and replacing the crankshaft is not, in itself, a terribly involved job but other resultant problems such as worn conrods rapidly complicate matters. Timing chains need to be changed every 20,000 miles because they stretch which, in the worst cases, will allow the engine to jump links with disastrous and very expensive results.

A worn timing chain can be detected by a rattling noise which will be present when the car is first started but will then disappear. Replacements can be bought for £45. Worn head gaskets will be indicated by overheating, water loss and pressurisation of the cooling system while a worn crankshaft will exhibit the characteristic knocking. None of these is disastrous in itself but the problem is knowing how long they have been like it and what other damage has been caused. It's a real guessing game!

It is wise to check for a reasonable service history and, if this is non-existent, it is best to assume the worst. It is also worth checking, if possible, that the garages involved with the car previously were well qualified to cope. The Stag engine was designed to fine tolerances which must be maintained and those working on them need to care about what they are doing if the job is to be a success.

One point worth mentioning here is that the Triumph Stag often falls victim to the 'engine swapper'. This was quite a popular activity a few years ago but these days, thankfully, the trend seems to be moving away from this idea and many of the specialists are now advising against it. It is easy to understand the thinking behind changing the engine for something a good deal more reliable but many owners underestimate the associated problems. The differing weights of the transplant units necessitate suspension and brake alterations which, if not undertaken correctly, can make the car positively dangerous. 'Foreign' engines which you are likely to find lurking within a Stag include the Triumph straight-six 2,498cc, the Rover V8 3,528cc and the trusty Ford 2,994cc V6.

Engine parts are not cheap due to their rarity and the fact that many have been remanufactured. If the car that you are inspecting has not had any verifiable engine rebuild work carried out within the past 50,000 miles you should beware. It is almost certain that, if this is the case, you will have to set aside at least £1,500 for mechanical work some time in the first two years of ownership.

Interior

Scimitars were nicely instrumented if not terribly ergonomic. Vacuum formed trim poses a repair problem but such as GRP replacement dashes are now available from specialists.

Stag interiors sometimes get rough treatment which can leave them rather the worse for wear. Seat cover re-trim kits are now available and cost about £70 (Mk 2).

— Scimitar

The GTE was a specialist car produced in small numbers so it is little wonder that a majority of original new parts are unavailable. Posing particular problems are the vacuum-formed trim panels of later cars which are almost impossible to repair when they crack (which they do). Specialist firms are taking this situation in hand and are reproducing such as dashboards in glassfibre but, as with the bodywork, a good interior should be rated over mechanical deficiencies when buying a Scimitar.

— Stag

In some cases the interior may have been chopped about with new accessories being added and even the seats changed. Returning it to standard can be an expensive business so it is best to check that it is all there in the first place. Some important parts are still only available as secondhand items which can make replacement difficult. ☐

The Specialists

Though produced in relatively small numbers, the Stag and Scimitar have a good specialist back-up.

In no particular order, here are some of the firms which look after these cars:

Scimitar

Graham Walker started a mail-order sevice for Scimitars in 1977 — now Cheshire-based **Graham Walker Ltd** are the largest sole dealers for Scimitar parts and are dealers for new Scimitars too (0244 851144). Their bulky parts catalogue is well worth obtaining for a start. The **Attleborough Scimitar Centre** is in Norfolk (0953 455556) and, well established, offers a wide range of Scimitar parts from stainless steel exhaust systems to recon. racks; **G.B. Black** of Leicester (0533 24383) has owned Scimitars for 13 years and carries out servicing and repairs; **Warmlake Engineering** of Maidstone look after sports cars generally but specialise in mechanical repairs to Scimitars *and* Stags. **Mike Hetherington** operates a spares service for Scimitars (and some Sabre parts) from Wakefield, Yorks (0924 252766).

Scimpart are, of course, Don Pither's company and sell an extremely wide range of spares for the four-wheel Reliants coupled with a remanufacturing service on certain lines (0452 863556). **Robin Rew**, like Don, cut his teeth on racing Sabres and now, appropriately, works from Silverstone (0327 857903) where he carries out all types of mechanical tasks, including modifications, for Scimitar owners. **Queensberry Road Garage** are yet another very established Scimitar specialist, but offer sales and spares as well as servicing/repairs (0536 513351).

J.W. Milward (Suffolk Scimitar Specialists) are Reliant main dealers and still carry parts for, and service, all SE5 and SE6 cars (0638 662087); **Will Sparrow Ltd** (0789 763656) are also Reliant main dealers and this Alcester company describe themselves simply as 'everything Scimitar', which includes restoration, sales, spares and servicing. **Nigel Newth-Gibbs** is Essex based (Purfleet 867900) with engines, chassis reconditioning, prop shafts and wire wheels among his specialities. **TC Improvements** are run by Terry Cox (0452 853556) who 'improves' Scimitar mechanics, chassis and bodywork. **TR Bitz** (0925 75 6841) can, because of Reliant's Triumph connection, supply suspension parts and a range of exhausts too.

Peter Smith Sportscars Ltd of Derby (0283 813593) claim to be the largest stockist of genuine Scimitar parts in the UK, and also buy, sell, service and repair Scimitars. **Chameeion Carriage Co.** hail from East Sussex (058087 622) also carry out a full range of work including GRP repairs, and buy and sell too. **Rickmansworth Sports Cars** are Scimitar main dealers and supply parts and services for GTE and GTC (0923 777040).

Stag

Rimmer Bros. (0522 791965) are now very heavily into Stags and can supply almost everything from exchange engines to Mk 1 facia sets; an SAE will bring you an extensive list. **Carlow Engineering** (0268 792817) Essex based and is run by Tony Carlow Bunton — they claim to have rebuilt no fewer than 106 Stag engines in the past 20 months! All mechanical work is taken on with considerable emphasis on engineering-out some of the Stag's design faults. **S.O.C. Spares Ltd** are official suppliers to the Stag Owners Club though independent of the club; a wide range of parts is available and you can apply for a useful catalogue (0622 842612) from this BL Heritage approved supplier.

H.R.S. Garages in London are one of the best-known 'Stag' names, Tony Hart being president of the Stag Owners Club; they also have BL Heritage approval and offer virtually every possible service a Stag owner could require. **Jerry Farrance** of Weston-Super-Mare (0934 26776) specialise in tuning and 'sorting' Stag (and Triumph) engines, plus gearbox and axle overhauls; they have a body shop too. **James Paddock** of Chester (0244 676827) offers a full service to Stag owners including restorations servicing and spares. **S.N.G. Barratt** are at Wolverhampton, are BL Heritage approved suppliers and carry a complete range of BL and 'pattern' Stag parts. **The Midland Stag Centre** with over 12 years, Stag experience offer a full service to Stag owners — speak to Ken Clarke on 0926 316306.

The Stag Workshop is Poole based (0202 747338) and Peter Edwards has specialised in Triumphs for many years; the firm repair and restore Stags, sell them and supply an 'own make' big-capacity Stag radiator. **The Hurley Motor Co.** are strictly 'transplant' people, replacing the Triumph V8 with brand-new ex-factory Ford V6s or Rover V8s (0203 661357); **Specialised Engines** of Grays, Essex (0375 378606) do the same but stick with the Ford V6, modified or standard. **The Stag Centre**, who are located in London E2 (01-739 7052/1344) have been in business for 10 years. They have amassed a considerable stock of new and secondhand parts and their full workshop facilities (including a rolling road), can cater for all requirements. **Peak Performance Cars** of Harlington, Essex (01-759 0828) have been specialising in Triumph Stags for many years and can offer one of the widest selections of secondhand cars available for sale in this country. Their spares stock is comprehensive and they are more than happy to talk to and advise Stag owners and potential owners who seek their assistance. Restoration and accident repair services are also offered.

And now the book....

If your appetite for Scimitars at least has been whetted by our issue this month, you'll be keen to read the new (and only) book on the subject which has just been published. It's called 'The Scimitar and its Forebears' and has been written by a true expert in the subject, Don Pither.

The 232-page book commences with Reliant's three-wheeler origins and traces the evolution of the marque through the Sabre, the Ogle connection and the first Scimitar coupe, the GTE and drophead, and the SS1. It is all highly readable and contains a wide variety of photographs, many of which are unusual and, of course, include the marque's sporting appearances. The technical descriptions of the cars are detailed and Don certainly doesn't neglect to compare each Reliant with its rivals — nor does he attempt

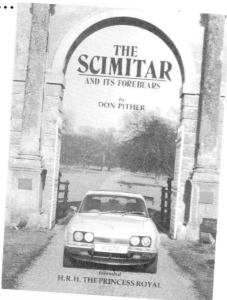

to disguise their faults while highlighting their virtues. The Appendices are very useful with full specifications, chassis number sequences, and even a 'GTE Family Tree' included. Don Pither does not count himself a professional author but certainly this book shows he can — on the subject of Reliant at least! — turn out a very professional product. He even managed to persuade H.R.H. Princess Anne — a longstanding GTE enthusiast — to contribute a foreword!

As a 'special offer' to *Practical Classics* readers Don has kindly arranged that the book can be ordered post-free until January 20 1988, saving £1.55 — your cheque for £11.95 should be made out to Court Publications and sent to them at Droys Court, Witcombe, Glos. GL3 4TN (allow 14 days for delivery).

P.O.S.

Stag Scimitar prices

	Cond 1	Cond 2	Cond 3
Stag Mk 1/2	£5,000	£2,500	£1,000
Scimitar SE5	£2,300	£1,400	£500
Scimitar SE5a	£3,100	£1,600	£700
Scimitar SE6	£3,000	£1,500	£1,100
Scimitar SE6a	£3,800	£2,400	£1,500
Scimitar SE6b	£6,500	£4,900	£3,200

NB: Concours-prepared vehicles can fetch considerably more than the above Condition 1 first-class order cars, particularly in the case of Stags. Mk 1 Stags, rarer than Mk 2s, are possibly appreciating faster. Note that for Scimitar SE6b cars, value is still affected by normal used-car age/mileage factors (our listings in the Price Guide are for mid-range examples).

Current values for Stags and GTEs are shown above; although not in our brief, Scimitar V6 coupe prices are between SE5 and 5a values with the straight-six (SE4) version considerably less (in our view, a really good SE4 of any type represents the best Scimitar for investment purposes). Earlier GTEs are still obtainable for well under £2,000 but if you buy in this category, be prepared for considerable work and expenditure if you want to end up with a top-bracket car. SE6bs are still governed by normal used-car depreciation factors so short term, you will lose money if you buy a late-model GTE. This is possibly true of the open SE8b but the market for open sporting cars being what it is, the GTC (442 built) will surely maintain its value

much better. Overall the picture is that, late models apart, GTE prices have stopped falling and are definitely on the upturn at last as enthusiasts actively seek out good SE5s and 6s.

On the other hand, the tide turned for the Stag some considerable time ago and while the cost of engine rectification and rust repairs has limited the rise in price of sub-standard examples, for mint original and properly rebuilt Stags the ceiling has recently approached the £8,000 mark. A few excep-tional cars have even exceeded this bench-mark but, as that means straying into Jaguar 'E' type territory, a further escalation is thought by some observers to be unlikely and that the price differential between Stags and open 'E' types will not be closed much further. As a generalisation though, and looking at the GTE and Stag in purely invest-ment terms, the Stag must be the more likely to show true appreciation over the next few years if only because it's an open car. The GTE's day is yet to come. □

Our thanks to......

The Reliant Sabre and Scimitar Owners Club; especially officials David Womack, Don Pither and Robin Rew — and members Mike Wollacott (whose SE6a features on our cover) and Ken Tape (owner of the white coupe seen in this feature); the Stag Owners Club; especially Richard Treacher, Publicity Officer; Club Triumph Eastern, especially Phil Taylor who made available his black Stag for photography; Pipps Hill Country Park, Basildon, for allowing us to use their patio for our 'shoot'; and all the major Stag and Scimitar specialists who helped us with information on every aspect of running the cars.

Thinking Of Buying A Scimitar..?

*John Williams takes a look and decides
that they make a good proposition.*

Classic car enthusiasts are rather like a group of people comparing operation scars and gleefully telling ever more gloomy tales about their health problems — we sometimes seem to take delight in the difficulty of getting parts, the ravages of rust, the thirst for petrol and the various other problems our chosen classic is prone to. In such a climate perhaps the Reliant Scimitars are a little too easy to live

The pre-1975 Scimitars described in this article can still provide fast motoring with a high degree of comfort, even luxury, but while their prices remain 'sensible' it is advisable to search for a genuinely sound example.

with, a shade too practical and just too logical a choice for some of us.

Supporters of glass-fibre bodywork and separate chassis construction like to give the impression that this is the ideal recipe for an almost everlasting motor-car and in the case of the Scimitars, barring accidents of a serious

nature, they are not far wrong. The performance, economy and handling of the Scimitars have always been praised although it should be added that there are some snags.

Our experience of the cars is that the Ford engine, particularly the V-6, and gearbox are not always as convenient to work on as they might be, located as they are, well back and low in the car. The interiors can deteriorate to the point of scruffiness in normal use and the GTE is no substitute for a furniture van, having very limited load-carrying space and rear seating best suited to children who like sitting still. A further disadvantage is that you do not have to look far to discover cars that have been treated as if they would last for ever on a diet of total neglect and high mileage, without any regard for the Scimitar's above average performance potential.

Many of the snags mentioned relate to badly looked-after cars and it should be mentioned that for such a "sensible" motor-car the Scimitar has many very pleasant characteristics — something which cannot be said of all cars. The lasting impressions are of the cars' long stride, balanced handling and

Only about 1000 of the Scimitar GT (usually described as the Coupe) were made, but the combination of a glass fibre body on a very sturdy chassis has helped to ensure that a few hundred survive.

Buying A

The temptation to own the relatively scarce Coupe must be balanced against the high cost of restoration work particularly if the interior is showing its age.

A factory option on the Coupe was a sliding roof although this example may have been a later modification.

Continued

relative economy in terms of maintenance as well as fuel consumption. All in all the Scimitars have much to recommend them.

What to look for.

Star crazing on the bodywork is not necessarily a serious matter but if there is actual (accident) damage or evidence of body repairs it is worth carrying out a thorough examination of the chassis. The chassis itself is extremely sturdy and the rust-prone areas are usually restricted to outriggers, the rear suspension bracing, and the outer chassis rails which run beneath the body sills.

Under the bonnet check for signs of water leaks and overheating, for example a leaking header tank in the Coupe or expansion tank in the GTE. The sensor bulb for the electric fan in the GTE merely pushes into a grommet in the radiator — and can equally easily pop out — so make sure that a retaining clip has been fitted. Inlet manifold gaskets deteriorate over a period of time and allow water to escape, a symptom of this being water lying on the top

The early coupes used the straight six 2½ litre Ford engine; subsequent models used 'V engines of 2½ and 3 litres. Engine compartments are well filled and the heater is located in the bulkhead behind the air cleaner.

Specifications and performance

Model	SE4 + SE4A	SE4B	SE4C	SE5	SE5A
Bore (mm)	82.6	93.67	93.67	93.67	93.67
Stroke (mm)	79.5	72.42	72.42	72.42	72.42
Capacity (cc)	2553	2994	2495	2994	2994
BHP	120	128	119	128	138
RPM	5000	4500		4750	5000
Length	14' 0''			14' 2¼''	
Width	5' 2¾''			5' 5''	
Weight (cwt)	21½	22	22	22½	22½
0-50 mph (secs)	8	7.2	8.7	7.7	8
0-60 (secs)	11.4	10	12.3	10.2	10.8
Max. speed (mph)	117	121	111	110	121
Fuel consumption (mpg)	20	22	20	19	23

Identification and model changes.

Date	Chassis Number	Series	Total Produced	Details
1964 September	SC 400001	SE4	59	Reliant Scimitar GT introduced. Overdrive optional.
	SC 400059	SE4A	237	Rear suspension location changed to two trailing arms per side and transverse Watts linkage.
1966 October	SC 400297			Last car with the straight six engine.
	SC 400401	SE4B	590	V6 3 litre engine introduced with new gearbox, disc wheels, new interior styling, improved ventilation and demisting.
1967 August	SC 425001	SE4C	117	V6 engined 2½ litre models introduced.
1968 August	SC 400901			Revised wheels, front suspension and interior trim.
1970 November	SC 400991			Final 3 litre GT.
	SC425118			Final 2½ litre GT.
1968 October	SC 450001	SE5	4029	First Scimitar GTE. Overdrive optional.
1969 October	SC 450500			Rear screen wiper/washers standardised. Automatic transmission optional, higher axle ratio on standard cars.
1971 September	SC 452501			Overdrive standard, redesigned interior, new heating and ventilating system, electric fan fitted.
1972 June	SC 453501			Uprated 3 litre engine fitted.
September	SC 454030			End of original chassis number sequence.
	93/1001			First of new chassis numbers.
1972 October	93/3422			Final number of this sequence (estimated).
	93X/3501	SE5A	8000	Another new chassis number sequence.
1975				SE5A series discontinued, SE6 models introduced at the Motor Show but cars did not reach the market until late in 1976.

of the engine having escaped up bolt holes. Many a cylinder head gasket has been changed in an effort to stop such leaks when it was the inlet manifold gasket that was at fault.

The top of the petrol tank also rusts but replacement tanks are available in either stainless or mild steel, and before fitting a new tank it is well worth using a petrol tank sealant. The rust-prone areas on the chassis can usually be repaired without disturbing the bodywork, but expert advice should be sought before proceeding — there are fire risks.

Scimitar..?

The coupe interior is compact and well finished with a complete range of instruments.

The coupe accomodation is of the '+2' variety with very limited legroom for adults . . .

. . . but there is a usable amount of boot space extending to just under the rear window.

The GTE is a much roomier car with seating for four adults plus useful luggage space. The pressed steel wheels wear bolt-on glass fibre embellishers from Reliant, alloy wheels were optional.

Access to the rear of the GTE is easy and either or both rear seats can be folded flat to provide the desired combination of seating and luggage space, but carrying capacity is limited by the size of the tail-gate.

What to pay

Most Scimitars do not receive as much maintenance as they should, partly because short of accident damage the good appearance of the bodywork lasts well and unless there are mechanical breakdowns it is easy to imagine that little maintenance is needed. It is worth spending as much money as you can to buy the best possible example. Although prices for both the GTE and the Coupe can start as low as £300-£400 such cars will require a lot of work and will probably cost more in the end than a genuinely sound example, costing £1,500 (or more) for the Coupe or around £2,000 for the GTE. Later GTEs (1976 onwards) which are not covered by this article are still valued as conventional secondhand cars and command higher prices.

The GTE interior offers more elbow and legroom and later cars (from about 1972) had more stylish but poorer quality interiors which are already showing signs of age with sagging and split dash panels, broken seat frames etc, though spares (if only second-hand) are available.

At 70,000 miles all the bearings and piston rings and the oil pump and its drive should be replaced; the engine should then be good for a further 50,000 miles. The oil pump drive is a hexagonal rod and once the ends become burred it will wear quickly and can lead to serious engine problems. Failure of the oil pump drive is particularly likely to happen when the engine is started in cold weather. In such conditions the engine runs quickly whilst the choke is applied, but the oil is thick and puts a heavy load on the oil pump. The oil pump drive fails, but the engine will continue to run, rapidly damaging bearings etc.

Gearboxes rarely give trouble unless abused although the change itself can be awkward and noisy compared with later Ford boxes. The GTE axle is strong but prone to pinion oil seal leaks leading to low oil level and increased wear. Some whine from the axle seems normal but if you buy a car which is fairly quiet in this respect it is well worth fitting a new oil seal and changing the axle oil. Also ensure that the breather hole on top of the righthand axle tube is not blocked, as this will cause a build-up of pressure which will overcome even a new oil seal. On any Scimitar you ignore a pool of oil under the rear axle at your peril. The Coupe axle is not as strong and the car should therefore be driven with rather less abandon, especially from a standing start. Spares for the Coupe and early GTE axles are now difficult to obtain.

It is worth checking the shock absorbers (the 'bounce' check will indicate their general condition) and you would be well advised to examine the front suspension carefully. Jack the car under the bottom wishbone to take the load off the suspension components so that you can check for wear in the vertical links and trunnions. Lack of grease, or grease emerging from the bottom of each trunnion will indicate expensive work, £50-£60 on each side in parts alone. All front suspension parts are readily

Buying A Scimitar..?

Much of the GTE engine compartment is filled by the spare wheel which is heavy and awkward to remove.

This is the oil pump drive showing evidence of the wear which is described in the text.

All Scimitars were built on very sturdy chassis, but rust can still be a problem and this will be apparent first in outriggers such as this one at the rear of the front wheel arch, and in the rails which run under tha edges of the body . . .

. . . and also under the rear wheel arches as shown in this picture.

On the GTE, cracks in the glass fibre of the inner wing, just behind the battery box, indicate that the bodywork (plus the spare wheel and radiator) forward of the suspension mounting posts is no longer adequately supported — the corrosion which weakens the metal structures supporting the body will be well hidden with the engine in situ.

The fire hazard associated with Scimitars was caused by the metal fuel pipe working loose and freeing itself from the carburettor, which allowed petrol to be sprayed over the engine and distributor. This is prevented by pinning the pipe into the carburettor (arrowed) and this should be done by a Reliant specialist.

Continued

available except for the vertical links on the early Coupe, but these cars can be converted to the later system. It is a good idea to ignore the over-long lubrication intervals recommended in the handbook and grease the front suspension every 1,000 miles instead.

The Coupe interior should be examined for wear due to age etc, bearing in mind the cost of interior renovations these days, but the GTE interior may well also show signs of dampness due to water leaks from any or all of the following; windscreen, gutters, rear side windows and tailgate. This creates a fairly unhealthy environment for carpets and interior trim in general and the only real solution is to fit new seals and/or quantities of sealing compound. Later Scimitars from about 1972 had poorer quality interiors which are already showing signs of age with split and sagging dash panels, broken seat frames etc, but spares are available. ☐

The writer wishes to thank Mr Peter Rix of the Lenham Motor Company Limited for his assistance in the preparation of this article.

Scimitar Servo Overhaul

Our Reliant Scimitar GTE (model SE5) was fitted with a Girling Powerstop Mk 2b (earlier models had the Mk 2a), but many other cars were fitted with these servos either as standard equipment or as optional extras.

Girling Powerstop servos were fitted to a large number of cars as standard equipment and were available as optional extras for a number of other vehicles too. The Mk 2b Powerstop servo was produced in two sizes, approximately 5½" and 7", these dimensions being the diameter of the vacuum chamber. The 5½" type was designed to provide a boost ratio of 1.56:1 or 2.04:1, and the 7" models 2.04:1 or 2.78:1. There were further variations

Overhaul is fairly straightforward if carried out methodically. It is worth taking care to place components on the bench in the exact order in which they are dismantled so that each part will be refitted in the correct order and the right way round.

Points to watch when overhauling the widely used Girling Powerstop unit, by John Williams.

The service kits (cost — about £25) contained everything we needed for the actual servo, but it was necessary to renew the vacuum hose from the servo to the inlet manifold, not surprising considering the amount of brake fluid that had escaped along that hose, helping it to collapse internally and become partly blocked — it proved to be water hose anyway which is not a satisfactory substitute even when in good condition.

Diminishing braking efficiency and a cloud of white exhaust smoke when accelerating are characteristic symptoms of an internal leak in a brake vacuum servo, the leaking hydraulic fluid finding its way into the engine via the inlet manifold which is connected to the servo in order to 'supply' the vacuum. Our 1973 Reliant Scimitar GTE, which is used by Bob Ashby,

recently developed this problem and we had the choice of replacing the Girling Powerstop servo unit or of overhauling it using a service kit which is readily available. A replacement unit would have cost as much as £80-£140 (or as little as £40 had we wanted one a week or so earlier — it certainly pays to 'shop around' and indeed to grab the bargains while you can).

dependent upon the position and type of non-return valve. The Mk 2a Powerstop was similar (although superseded by the Mk 2b) and this article should also be helpful to owners of this type. Clearly it is important to confirm the precise identity of your servo before ordering the service kit, as internal components vary slightly in number and size, and it is equally important whilst carrying out the overhaul to compare old and new components carefully as some items (especially rubber seals) could be easily confused and fitted in the wrong places.

Our picture captions should be read in conjunction with the service kit instructions which were detailed and clear. Cleanliness is vital when handling hydraulic components,

especially when reassembling the new parts and we placed the service kit components on a sheet of white paper and added other parts which were to be replaced only after they had been cleaned. The service kit instructions state that a support plate is required so that the servo can be held in a vice during the overhaul. The dimensions of the support plate are supplied, but Ted Landon removed the servo from the car complete with the bracket by which it is attached to the inner wing panel and we were able to secure the assembly in a vice without causing damage to the servo casting.

The only component which gave us difficulties during dismantling was the plug adjacent to the control piston. This is a solid cylindrical plug with a slot around its perimeter which houses a rubber seal. It is a close fit in the end of the control piston bore, and ours could not be pushed out as indicated by the instructions. We succeeded eventually by using a hammer and drift to knock the plug further into the bore (about 1/8" further), and after cleaning and lubricating the end of the bore with fresh hydraulic fluid we found that the plug could indeed be pushed out by using a bent rod inserted through the 'T' lever aperture to push the control piston against the inner face of the plug.

Undo the two Philips screws to release the lever guide and spring plate (arrowed) . . . .

. . . and the 'T' lever and two valves can be pulled out, although it may be necessary to depress the plug in the control piston aperture to release the 'T' lever.

A long piece of vacuum hose is needed to connect the servo (when in the vice) to the inlet manifold (arrowed) as it is necessary to run the engine in order to create vacuum in the servo during dismantling and again when reassembling the vacuum chamber. Do not underestimate the dangers from exhaust gases but leave the garage doors open, at least while the engine is running.

Before the front and rear shells of the vacuum chamber are separated it is necessary to release the cover of the valve chest (or separate the rubber sleeve, arrowed, from the pipe leading to the valve chest) whilst holding the shells together to prevent the rear shell from flying off due to the spring inside. Then stand clear as you separate the shells so that any brake fluid in the vacuum chamber can spill without getting on your clothes.

The plug mentioned in the previous caption is arrowed here and must be removed (as described in the text) to gain access to the control piston . . . .

The two shells which form the vacuum should be reassembled in the same relative position, so scribe a line across them before they are separated. The clamping ring which secured the shells on our Mk 2b Powerstop servo was released by sawing through the small metal plate welded to it. The procedure is different on the Mk 2A model which has a bolt-on flat cover.

When removing the three setscrews and the clamping plate in the rear shell beware of the possibility of the output piston and adjacent parts flying out of its bore under spring pressure. Ours was firmly restrained by the bush — which is being prised out in this picture. Make sure that you retrieve the ball bearing which is part of the output piston assembly — we found re-assembly easier with the new ball bearing uppermost on the valve and the valve bore horizontal as shown here.

. . . which can then be withdrawn as an assembly and dismantled on the bench.

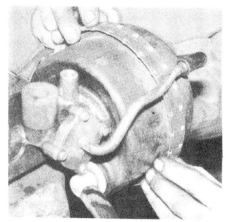

When re-assembling the vacuum chamber, vacuum created by the engine is used to draw the two shells together in their original relative positions while the service clamping ring is fitted. Do not rush this part of the job but ensure that the V pressings on the ring are all correctly positioned in relation to the edges of the shells.

A servo which is clearly faulty needs to be overhauled, but bear in mind that braking systems can suffer from many other defects which reduce efficiency, that a lack of vacuum at the inlet manifold will affect the entire system — and no amount of work on the brakes will put that right. Or the original problem may be due to a simple blockage in the pipe from the inlet manifold to the servo, which may not be apparent from the external appearance of that pipe.

Having refitted the servo in the engine compartment and reconnected the two hydraulic pipes and renewed the vacuum pipe to the inlet manifold it will then be necessary to bleed the brakes.

Reliant Scimitar
Part One

Geoff Le Prevost starts our Scimitar rebuild with the restoration of the Ford 3 litre engine

Scimitar/Ford V6 Engine Rebuild

There are two Ford V6 engines. One of 2.8 litres and known as the German unit, and the other of 2.5 or three litres, home grown and sometimes known as the British V6. It is the three litre motor that we have been looking at. It first appeared in the manufacturer's Mk IV Zephyr/Zodiac in 1966 and subsequently powered several other 'big' Fords. It was also to be found heading up the drive train of a wide variety of semi-exotics from specialist manufacturers who appreciated the good power to money ratio offered by this readily available unit.

The engine powered the Gilbern Genie and Invader, the Marcos Three Litre, the TVR Tuscan and later 3000M as well as the similarly named AC 3000ME and, of course, the Reliant Scimitar GTE, an example of which has been with the *Practical Classics* staff fleet

for some time. The car was in constant hard use covering about 30,000 miles in just over a year before being placed on the 'reserve' list. The Scimitar clocked up 100,000 miles just recently and, with its now very low mileage reading, it seemed like a good time to rebuild the motor.

We should point out, right from the start, that if you have a tired old V6 and you want to revitalise your car, then by far the cheapest line of action is to invest in an exchange unit. You should bear in mind, however, that exchange engines vary greatly in quality from the 'scrapyard special' taken straight out of an old or damaged car, to the totally reconditioned motor built with all-new parts. The

The lower rocker is as it came off the car, the upper one has been lightly burnished and shows no sign of pitting.

The valves showed a typical reaction to high mileage but valve guides were OK.

Scimitar/Ford V6 Engine Rebuild
C O N T I N U E D

Core plugs should always be replaced. The old plug, lower right, shows signs of decay and imminent failure.

problem, of course, is that you cannot always tell what you are getting.

Our target was to return the Scimitar to the category of reliable workhorse, capable of giving us another 30,000 miles in one year. To achieve this, we elected to do the job the expensive way — by having it stripped and carefully rebuilt using new components wherever necessary.

We asked our Beckenham-based mechanic Eric Gilbert to carry out the work and, in getting the components together, he was able to use his experience in the trade to shop around for the best buys, but there is nothing preventing you from doing the same. All the internal parts of the engine are standard Ford so there are no problems with availability. If you choose to rebuild your own unit and, like us, find that most components need replacing, expect a parts-only bill of around £450.

The Ford V6 is an all-steel unit and therefore very heavy so, whatever car you are

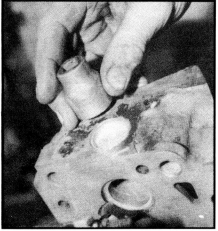

The core plug can be inserted using an old socket of suitable size.

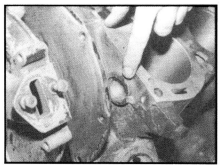

This core plug hides behind the engine front plate and must be changed.

removing the engine from, you will need heavy-duty lifting gear. Eric totally dismantled the unit and in this and the next issue of *Practical Classics* we will be following the reassembly.

There was nothing innovative in the design of this engine so there should be little to baffle the competent DIY rebuilder but a workshop manual will earn its keep in the otherwise average tool kit.

The top end of the engine is totally conventional. The valves are operated by horrible but effective rocker arms and push rods from a single camshaft mounted centrally in the top of the block. The heads are identical and therefore interchangeable. It is a good idea to put everything back where it came from, so replacing the alternator bracket fixing bolt in one head will tell you that this is front and right. While the block was being re-bored (of which more later) work started on the top end.

The heads were cleaned and checked for distortion by fogging them with a spray lubricant like WD40, then lightly running fine emery cloth, wrapped around a known straight edged block of wood, across the faces (the matching faces on the block had also been checked). If you are in any doubt, consult your local engineer about re-facing. With the valves still in place, the combustion chambers were cleaned using a wire brush in an electric drill. The heads were then dismantled fully, keeping each rocker arm and retaining nut assembly in partnership with its own pushrod — in this case, all laid out on a sheet of corrugated cardboard.

The valves can be removed using a valve spring compressor and the ports cleaned using a small wire brush in a drill — being careful not to damage the valve seatings or guides. The valves on our heads were very badly silted up and quite obviously required some attention.

You should note that the inlet valves have 'aluminised' heads and they should not be reground or lapped in. If they are worn or damaged they should be replaced. The exhaust valves do not have this protective coating so they can be re-ground and lapped.

When rebuilding any engine, it is vital to replace all of the core plugs — even though they may look sound. One or two of ours showed signs of weeping and they were all rusted to wafer thinness. It would be tragic to

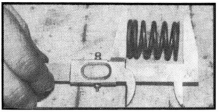

The old valve springs were a long way short of the workshop manual specified size. The spring should be fitted with the close-coiled end against the cylinder head.

Just how much work had to be done on the heads — shown in the contrast between the finished example and the one on which work has yet to start.

The rocker, the socket-like device on which it rocks, and the non-locking nut which can cause problems if it comes loose.

The push rods should be checked in their guides. There should be no play.

run a newly rebuild engine for a few miles and then lose coolant through a faulty core plug — particularly if the blown plug was one of the inaccessible ones requiring an engine out exercise to replace it.

The new or cleaned valves should be given a light coating of oil before refitting. This goes for all engine components. Some restor-

The top faces of the block were checked for true before the rebore.

One of the reasons for a rebore — a set of broken rings, as found.

ers like to see every engine part swimming in oil, others prefer to be neat and clean and to give just a sufficient coating of oil to provide lubrication until the motor's own oil delivery system comes in to play.

The valve springs should be checked for free length. Ours seemed shorter than the workshop manual specified, but the replacements — which we were assured most categorically were correct — were slightly short. It seems that there was a production specification change somewhere along the line. Always fit new oil seals to the valve stems, the old ones might look sound but they harden with age.

The rockers in our engine were savable; severe pitting on the valve stem contact face could make replacement necessary, though slight marking can be lightly ground down. The rockers are held in place by a single, non-locking nut which tends to be a loose fit even when new and which makes the tappets noisy and timing impossible. Eric likes to crimp these nuts lightly in a vice before fitting. This might sound a little rough, but there doesn't seem to be any other way to ensure tightening *and* adjustment.

The pushrods should be checked for fit in their guides. These guides are bolted in pairs to the head and there should be no sideways play — if there is, the top end of the engine will be noisy. The push rods have an oilway running up through the centre and this should be checked just to make sure it is clear.

The block, meanwhile, was being re-bored at Cedar Engineering in Penge. They also reground the crankshaft and supplied the appropriate pistons, a new oil pump (always worthwhile) and oil pump drive. We decided against a re-profiled cam shaft and bought a new one. We also bought a full set (12) of cam followers and, of course, a new fibre timing wheel. This wheel is one of the very few weak points of the Ford motor — and we'll go into more detail about that next month.

NEXT MONTH
Putting the engine back together again.

Reliant Scimitar
Part Two

Geoff Le Prevost reports on the final stages of rebuilding our Scimitar power plant.

Scimitar/Ford V6 Engine Rebuild

When Eric Gilbert stripped our 100,000 mile Scimitar engine, he found it in fairly good condition, bearing in mind a history of abuse and the usual Scimitar problem of over-heating. With the heads off, the bores didn't look too desperate, but when the pistons were removed, each and every one of them carried a broken ring. It is almost certain that damage on this sort of scale must have been inflicted when the engine was last overhauled some 30,000 miles earlier.

The block was sent to Cedar Engineering, in Penge, where it was rebored. The company also reground the crankshaft and supplied the matching bearings, supplied new pistons and rings and fitted them to the existing con rods, fitted new core plugs all round and fitted new camshaft bushes. They also supplied, separately, a set of gaskets and seals, an oil pump and an oil pump drive. We

also asked them to dunk the block in their degreasing bath.

The bill for this came to very nearly £300 proving, as I suggested last month, that there are cheaper ways to keep the car mobile than rebuilding the existing unit. However, this way we are *assured* of what is virtually a brand new engine and not many commercially available replacement units can boast that.

The difference in price between a repro-filed camshaft and a brand new unit was a matter of £10 or so. Reprofiling means taking metal off the lobes to compensate for wear until the original profile is reached, but with, obviously, a smaller lobe. We opted for a new cam shaft which is, incidently a standard

The four bearing halves correctly placed — note that each has an oil hole in the centre. It is all too easy to fit a blank shell and effectively block off the oil supply to that bearing.

Ford item like everything else within the engine casing. We added a full set of cam followers to the shopping list as the existing parts looked pretty 'cooked'.

If there is any deviation from the absolutely normal about the design of the V6, it is that timing chains have been dispensed with

Scimitar/Ford V6 Engine Rebuild

C O N T I N U E D

The crank can be protected with an oil spray until the time for rebuilding comes around.

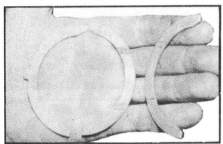

The thrust washers come in a variety of sizes and the machine shop which carries out the rebore/crank regrind will supply the right type.

and the task is carried out by a timing wheel with fibre teeth which sits on the end of the camshaft and engages with a steel gear wheel, half its size, on the crank shaft. The system works very well until the fibre teeth start to wear when the timing will suffer. It has been known for teeth to break and then you really are in trouble. So, if you are doing any sort of overhaul work, check the condition of the wheel as a matter of course.

Before Eric started the assembly work, he checked all of the oilways with an airline. If you have your own paint spray compressor, you can get accessories for it which include a small air gun. If you haven't a compressor, try a length of clean plastic tubing (or what about a plastic drinking straw?) and blow through it yourself.

When you are sure that the oilways are clear, inject fresh engine oil into the passages being very careful to check that there is no grit on the nozzle of your oil can. It pays to be surgically clean right through the assembly stages.

Main bearing caps come in three types, all with an arrow indicating 'front'. They are also marked F for front, C for centre and two seemingly identical caps (on our car at least) were marked R for rear. In the event, these two caps *weren't* identical and, on the first fitting, when they were torqued down, the crank wouldn't turn. We swapped the two similar caps and solved the problem. Do not forget that the shell main bearing halves are different — one half has a hole in the centre

The oil pick up filter holder was just about to drop off the pipe — so it was brazed in place.

The oil pump drive shaft has a spring clip near the end. This fits over the collar at the top of the pump.

The engine should be laid on its back plate to allow the camshaft to be lowered very carefully in to the block.

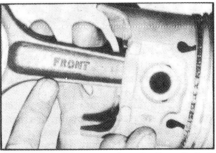

The pistons and the con rods are both marked, the pistons with an F and the rod with the word 'front' (indicated).

and the other half is plain. The shell with the hole is placed in the block to match the oilway; the plain shell goes in the bearing cap where there is no oilway.

If you have to wait a while between getting the crank reground (and, perhaps, the bearing in the front end replaced) and refitting it, it might be a good idea to coat it with a spray lubricant like WD40 — but remember to clean off the oil and the dust it will gather before refitting — then the reground surfaces will be as good as new.

Place the crank into the oiled shell bearings in the block then press the other bearing

A liberal dosing of oil will help the piston to slip into the bore. Once the rings are compressed, the piston can be lightly tapped using a piece of wood or a hammer handle.

There is a pin-hole oilway in the indentation indicated which sprays lubricant onto the timing wheels. It is vitally important that this is clear.

When the timing wheels have been correctly lined up, the clearance between the teeth should be checked.

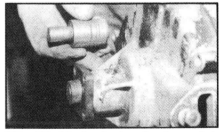

This odd looking bearing is an interference fit in the 'nose' of the front plate. The clip on the upper side of the surround has to be removed to free the bearing.

halves into the caps and place them onto the crank. Make sure the bolts are clean and the threads perfect before fitting. The thrust bearings are also in two halves and each has a plain side and a slotted side. The slots go to the crank and the plain sides to the main bearings. The pin on the top of one half slots into the main bearing cap. When everything is loosely fitted, tap the front and rear bearings to help settle them and then start tightening up the bolts, moving diagonally as you would when tightening cylinder head bolts, torqueing to the limits specified for your engine (check your workshop manual). It is not a bad idea to set the torque wrench to, say, half the required torque to start with, bring all the bolts up to this level, and then ease the pressure up gradually.

The rear crank seal should be drifted carefully from its alloy carrier and the carrier cleaned before fitting a new seal. A liberal application of grease might help to ease the new seal on to the crank. When fitting the carrier, rotate it to centralise it before fitting the bolts.

The big end bearings are sometimes covered in a preservative, so make sure thay are clean before fitting. Make sure the bearings are correctly fitted and slip the pistons into the bores using oil to ease the journey. Oil on the inside of the ring compressor will help to protect the piston rings. The big end caps have holes and the con rods have matching dowels, so you cannot fit them the wrong way around. Slip the camshaft very carefully into the block, being extra wary of not chipping a lobe.

There are at least three different types of oil pump. Check the new unit against the old if you are replacing the pump. Check also that the bolts you have are the right length. We replaced our pump as a matter of course — why take risks when the rest of the job has been so expensive? We also found that the pick up filter was just about to fall off the pick up pipe, so Eric brazed it back on.

Fit the timing gear and line up the timing marks. The engine will almost certainly be very stiff at this stage and you may need to use a socket and tommy bar on the retaining bolt of one of the timing wheels to turn the engine to the correct spot to line the timing marks up. Check the clearance between the teeth on the timing wheels with a feeler gauge. The workshop manual will specify the clearance for your engine.

With the sump on, we turned to the heads which Eric had overhauled while waiting for the block to return from the machine shop (see last month's *Practical Classics*). Remember to drop in the cam followers before you think about fitting the heads — you will not get the followers in with the heads on. You have been warned. The heads are held on with bolts so there are no studs to line up the mating surfaces — so Ford included spring dowels and when these are sprung into place in the bolt holes, the heads slip into place very easily.

With the head bolts torqued down, the push rods can be slid into place and the rockers fitted. The engine front plate can be fitted and it is worth checking that the top pulley bearing (it is a press fit into the 'nose' of the plate) is turning smoothly. To replace that bearing, remove the circlip on the side of the housing and drift the bearing out. Press the new bearing in and replace the clip.

In order to avoid working with 'messy' components, the timing wheels were put together 'dry' and then lubricated when the front cover was in place. The engine can be turned while oil is fed in through the fuel pump drive.

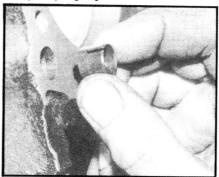

The heads are positioned on the block using the spring dowels.

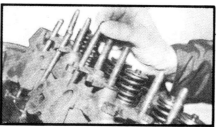

With the heads bolted down, the push rods can be slipped into place and the rocker assembly fitted.

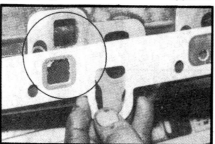

The manifold gasket can be correctly positioned by lining up the only square hole in the manifold face with the corresponding hole in the gasket (circled).

The manifold gasket can be held in place with a light application of grease or gasket compound while the manifold is being fitted.

The inlet manifold sits between the two heads and has a gasket which puzzles some fitters. There is only one way the gasket can be fitted, and that is to line up the one square hole in the manifold with the only square hole in the gasket.

Before we refit the engine, we'll be overhauling the gearbox, paying particular attention to the horrible mess of rods which make up the gear change linkage. We'll also be trying to make the overdrive unit work for the first time since we acquired the car. When the engine is finally put back in the car, we'll be checking the ancilliary components but it is worth mentioning that if you are refitting the original carburettor, do make sure the fuel line is secure. It is a common fault on Scimitars that this line falls off the carb, pumping fuel onto the top of a hot engine where it forms a pool and eventually ignites. I have it on fairly good authority that, when this happens, it takes about 30 seconds for a glass fibre Scimitar to be an end-to-end inferno — so have that fuel line professionally pinned onto the carb. □

NEXT MONTH
We investigate problems
in the transmission.

Reliant Scimitar
Part Three

The faults, the diagnosis and the repairs described by John Williams.

The next stage in the overhaul of our Reliant Scimitar GTE is the reassembly of the gearbox. Our Beckenham based engineer, Eric Gilbert, dismantled the gearbox some time ago in order to clean all the components thoroughly and examine them for wear and order the necessary replacements.

Whenever possible a gearbox should be "road tested" before dismantling commences in order to identify problems. A careful note of the problems — difficulty in selecting gears, jumping out of gear, noises in certain gears etc — will be most useful during dismantling, assisting the methodical worker in locating the worn components which are causing the problems.

Scimitar/Ford V6 Gearbox Rebuild

Tracing the faults

For example, if it is gear selection whilst the car is in motion which is the difficulty it is very likely that the brass synchromesh cones are worn and not exerting a sufficient braking effect on the tapers of the relevant gears. If jumping out of gear is a problem the fault lies

with a worn synchro hub associated with the affected gear. An abnormal noise in 1st, 2nd and 3rd gear but not in top gear suggests a problem associated with the layshaft (which is not under load when 4th gear is in use) such as worn thrust washers or damaged needle rollers. The causes of most problems can be

The gearbox assembly minus the selector mechanism and cover — absolute cleanliness is all important during reassembly particularly on an overdrive gearbox. Wear in bearings can be detected by hand, feel for free lateral movement and spin the bearing and listen for the "chattering" noise caused by wear or actual damage. Bearing should be thoroughly washed in paraffin before testing as oil residues disguise the evidence of wear.

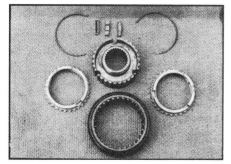

The 3rd/4th synchro hub dismantled — both this and the 1st/2nd gear synchro hub were sufficiently worn to justify replacement even at about £80 and £120 respectively, the latter is more expensive because it incorporates reverse gear.

isolated given a little thought and some prior knowledge of the problems. It would be a different matter if you were faced with a gearbox of unknown performance when your decisions as to which components should be replaced would have to be based solely upon an examination of the components. In this situation some previous experience of gearbox work would be desirable if not essential, not least because some components are very expensive, and gearboxes are not the most accessible items should you fail to replace enough components at the first attempt.

To a novice the gearbox may seem an extremely complicated assembly but a methodical beginner could certainly tackle the overhaul work on our box. Few tools are needed and nothing more "specialised" than a pair of circlip pliers, a brass drift, and sufficiently large spanner (preferably ring) to cope with the rear main bearing retaining nut.

Re-assembly

The reassembly of the input shaft and the main shaft components is covered in the picture captions.

The first component to be put back in the gearbox casing is the layshaft gear cluster complete with new needle roller bearings and a dummy layshaft. The dummy layshaft is

The layshaft gear cluster with spots of coloured paint (arrowed). The colour coding relates to the gear ratios — this box was used in a number of vehicles some of which employed different ratios.

We fitted new synchro hubs, and also new bearings throughout including layshaft needle bearings, thrust washers on the layshaft, new circlips throughout, a new locking tab washer (to eliminate risk of old one breaking and floating about in the gearbox), and a new reverse idler gear — the original one shown here displays wear on the gear teeth.

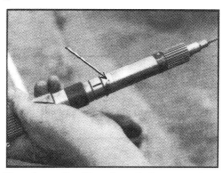

There is an oil gallery through the centre of the main shaft from its rear end to two holes about 4-5" from the end — here oil is being pumped into the gallery to ensure that it is clear (it can be seen emerging from one of the holes — arrowed) and to wash out any dirt within.

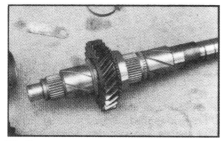

The first component to be fitted to the main shaft is second gear as shown here. A small amount of oil is applied to the shaft before each component is fitted and we used a little grease on the gear tapers in order to retain synchromesh cones. Note that in all of these pictures the direction of the front of the gearbox is to the left of the picture except where stated otherwise.

Next the brass baulk ring is fitted to the forward side of the 1st/2nd gear synchro hub and the hub fitted on the shaft behind 2nd gear. Then a circlip is fitted in a groove around the shaft as seen here — in this picture the forward end of the shaft is pointing downwards.

not absolutely vital but will make the job a great deal less troublesome. It should be the same diameter as the actual layshaft but shorter, in fact fractionally shorter than the layshaft gear cluster. New needle roller bearings (22 at each end) are inserted into the ends of the layshaft gear cluster and retained by some grease. When one set of bearings are in place the dummy layshaft can be inserted and the other set of bearings pushed in around the shaft. Count the bearings as you fit them to ensure that none is left out. The complete assembly is now laid in the bottom of the gearbox casing which in turn lies on its right side on the bench (it is the left side of this box rather than the top to which the main cover and selector assembly are fitted). At this stage you should also fit the thrust washers which locate in grooves in the casing by means of tabs and also have oil channels which should face the ends of the layshaft gear cluster. It will be virtually impossible to fit these later so use grease to hold them in place and then disturb the main casing as little as possible. Note that the larger thrust washer fits at the front of the casing adjacent to the largest gear on the layshaft cluster.

With the layshaft assembly loose in the gearbox casing the input shaft and bearing can be fitted in the aperture at the front of the gearbox until the circlip around the bearing is against the casing. The main shaft is now inserted from the rear of the casing not forgetting the roller bearing at its forward end which fits inside the rear end of the input shaft, and also the fourth gear baulk ring which, despite a smear of grease, will want to fall into the bottom of the box.

Next the layshaft cluster is lifted into position using a couple of lengths of stiff wire and the layshaft is inserted from the rear of the casing, simultaneously pushing out the dummy shaft which should ensure that none of the needle rollers is displaced. Finally the reverse gear idler shaft is also inserted from the rear of the box, fed through the idler gear and into the bracket within the box. Both of

Scimitar/Ford V6 Engine Rebuild
C O N T I N U E D

these shafts are keyed at their rear end and when fully home the keys should be in a horizontal position to line up with the slot in the first part of the overdrive casing. We will be working on the overdrive and selector mechanism soon and to hold the main shaft in position until then Eric fitted the first part of the overdrive casing complete with gasket,

stored in that order whilst being cleaned and examined. Newcomers to major mechanical tasks such as this would be well advised to keep notes and make sketches so that there are no mysteries as to how things fit (and nothing gets left out) during reassembly. It would be so easy to overlook circlips, baulk rings, and the fact that the 3rd/4th gear synchro hub has a groove around one of its outer tapers which should face the rear of the box. Compare new parts with old to make sure that they will fit without stretching and also without covering oil holes (like the one at the front of the box). This is a later box than the one shown in our Scimitar workshop manual. The cover and selector mechanism on the ear

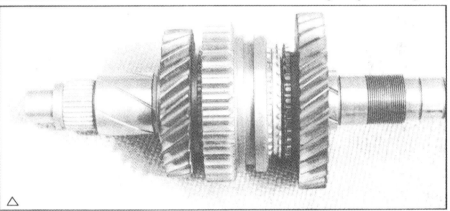

Then the 3rd/4th gear synchro hub complete with a baulk ring on either side is fitted to the shaft with the grooved outer part of the hub facing backwards. This synchro hub may need tapping along the shaft to clear the groove on the shaft which houses a circlip which is fitted next. This picture also shows the rear end of the input shaft complete with bearing and 4th gear (arrowed).

Now 1st gear (the large cog on the right in this picture) is fitted preceded by another baulk ring . . .

. . . followed by an oil scoop device which collects oil and directs it to the channels on the shaft below 1st gear. Note that the oil scoop must be fitted correctly as shown here with the open side of its oil galleries towards 1st gear, it also has a tooth on its inner perimeter which engages in a groove on the shaft.

noting that there is a locating dowel at the top centre of this component.

The front cover of the gearbox was fitted next complete with gasket and gasket sealant to minimise the risk of oil leaks. To protect

The front main bearing is pressed onto the input shaft with the open side of the bearing facing forward — but first check that the oil gallery in the shaft (which supplies the bearing) is clear. A circlip fits onto the shaft in front of the bearing and a large circlip fits the groove around the perimeter of the bearing.

Next the rear gearbox main bearing is fitted to the shaft. To achieve this the shaft is secured in a vice (Eric used an old synchro hub as a sleeve to protect the shaft from the vice) and the bearing retaining nut used to press bearing onto shaft (see the heading picture). Once the bearing was properly located the nut was removed and refitted using a new locking tab washer.
Third gear (arrowed) can now be added to the forward end of the main shaft, the taper on the gear assembly (on which fits the brass baulk ring) facing forward.

the oil seal from chafing on the input shaft splines Eric applied a large amount of grease to the splines (excess grease being removed afterwards), and suggested that tinfoil would be equally effective in protecting the seal.

I have not covered dismantling the box but clearly it should not be done haphazardly. There should be plenty of clear working space so that components can be laid out in the order in which they were dismantled and

Note that the gearbox front cover contains an oil seal and also has a cutaway channel in the flange through which oil which has passed through the bearing can return to the gearbox via a hole in the casing. This cover is fitted with the oil channel and also the drainage hole in the front sleeve pointing downwards.

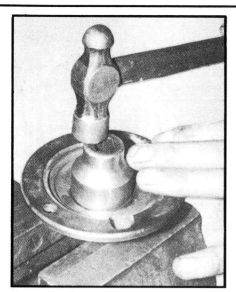

A new oil seal should be fitted to the front cover. The old seal is levered out and the new one tapped in squarely using a socket of suitable size to prevent distortion.

This picture shows the front end of the gearbox with the dummy layshaft (in Eric's left hand) being pushed out as the actual layshaft is inserted from the back of the box.

lier type of box is on top of the box and not on the left-hand side as in this instance. Parts are readily available if you have access to a Ford dealer and in this connection I would like to pay tribute to Keith at K.T. Dartford for his help.

The reverse idler gear shaft (arrowed) is also inserted through the rear of the box and fed through the gear and into the fixed bracket within the box. The rear ends of the layshaft and reverse idler gear shaft are shaped to fit a slot in the first part of the overdrive casing — we fitted this casing at this stage to hold the mainshaft in place whilst we attended to the selector mechanisms and the overdrive. Note that this casing has a locating dowel at centre top.

NEXT MONTH
The overdrive overhaul.

Reliant Scimitar
Part Four
Reassembly work described by John Williams.

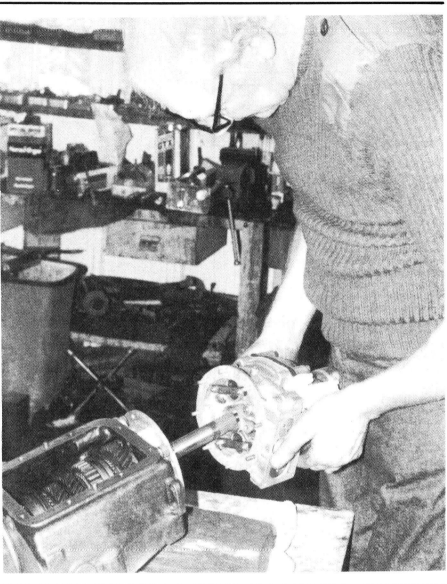

My method of tackling our mechanical overhaul stories tends to place the great emphasis on the reassembly work rather than on the dismantling. I often wonder whether this has anything to do with my childhood persuit of dismantling almost anything that I could get my hands on only to find that I could not work out how to put things together again. I have improved somewhat over the years. I have been known to use a pencil and notebook to record the dismantling operation, and have even employed a camera on occasions.

The important thing is that I have become convinced of the importance of keeping a detailed record when carrying out any unfamiliar dismantling job. Dismantling is

Scimitar/Laycock
Overdrive Rebuild

often very easy and it is equally easy to convince yourself that you will still remember the details next weekend (or whenever) when you intend to reassemble the component. The chances are that you will not remember but will find some notes, sketches etc, invaluable.

If it is a Laycock J type overdrive which you are trying to reasssemble you should find this feature helpful (whether you have your own notes or not). The overdrive from our Reliant Scimitar was overhauled by Eric Gilbert and he was keen to emphasise that he used no special tools, but employed methods

Scimitar/Laycock Overdrive Rebuild

C O N T I N U E D

If you have not tackled an overdrive before, this impressive array of parts need not put you off. It really is not as complicated an assembly as you may imagine and we found that re-assembly required no special tools.

Our first job was to fit the small bearing, (55) (which carries the end of the gearbox shaft) in the centre of the annulus (arrowed) and some bearing adhesive was used as we discovered that this bearing had 'escaped' during a previous reassembly and was loose in the overdrive. Then a thrust washer (56) was fitted.

which would be within the scope of the do-it-yourself enthusiast. Indeed it would be worth outlining Eric's method of working on this type of job; firstly he dismantles the component, cleans each part thoroughly using paraffin, and stores it in a suitable container (small parts or groups or related small parts can be stored together in plastic freezer bags and labelled). After a thorough cleaning the components are examined for wear and damage, and a list is made of the replacement parts needed.

The replacement parts are ordered and by the time that I arrive on the scene laden with cameras and tape recorder the new parts have arrived and all the original components will have been brought out of storage and laid out on an old kitchen table (in Eric's garage, or on the lawn on a fine day – I did point out ear-

lier that Eric tries to simulate the methods employed by the home restorer!), usually in the order of assembly and ready for an "exploded photograph".

Our Reliant Scimitar was fitted with a Laycock J type overdrive (fixed flange model) for which a service manual is still available from Laycock Engineering (contact

Laycock Overdrive Fixed Flange Model

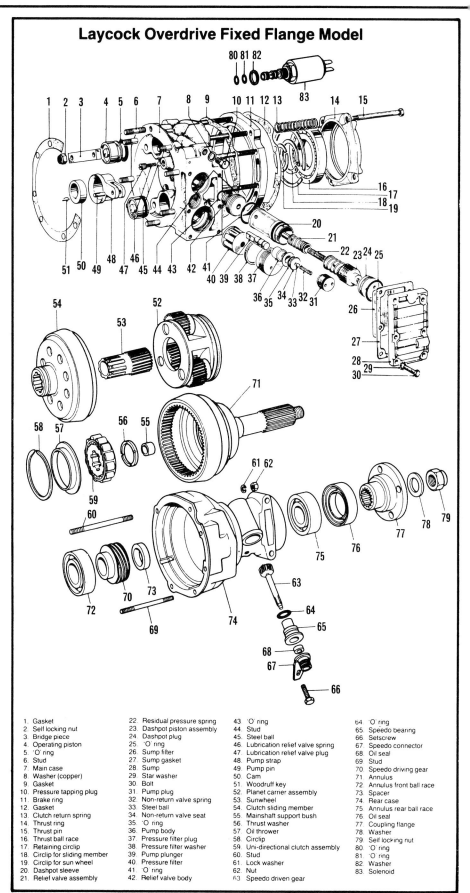

1. Gasket	22. Residual pressure spring	43. 'O' ring
2. Self locking nut	23. Dashpot piston assembly	44. Stud
3. Bridge piece	24. Dashpot plug	45. Steel ball
4. Operating piston	25. 'O' ring	46. Lubrication relief valve spring
5. 'O' ring	26. Sump filter	47. Lubrication relief valve plug
6. Stud	27. Sump gasket	48. Pump strap
7. Main case	28. Sump	49. Pump pin
8. Washer (copper)	29. Star washer	50. Cam
9. Gasket	30. Bolt	51. Woodruff key
10. Pressure tapping plug	31. Pump plug	52. Planet carrier assembly
11. Brake ring	32. Non-return valve spring	53. Sunwheel
12. Gasket	33. Steel ball	54. Clutch sliding member
13. Clutch return spring	34. Non-return valve seat	55. Mainshaft support bush
14. Thrust ring	35. 'O' ring	56. Thrust washer
15. Thrust pin	36. Pump body	57. Oil thrower
16. Thrust ball race	37. Pressure filter plug	58. Circlip
17. Retaining circlip	38. Pressure filter washer	59. Uni-directional clutch assembly
18. Circlip for sliding member	39. Pump plunger	60. Stud
19. Circlip for sun wheel	40. Pressure filter	61. Lock washer
20. Dashpot sleeve	41. 'O' ring	62. Nut
21. Relief valve assembly	42. Relief valve body	63. Speedo driven gear

64. 'O' ring	
65. Speedo bearing	
66. Setscrew	
67. Speedo connector	
68. Oil seal	
69. Stud	
70. Speedo driving gear	
71. Annulus	
72. Annulus front ball race	
73. Spacer	
74. Rear case	
75. Annulus rear ball race	
76. Oil seal	
77. Coupling flange	
78. Washer	
79. Self locking nut	
80. 'O' ring	
81. 'O' ring	
82. Washer	
83. Solenoid	

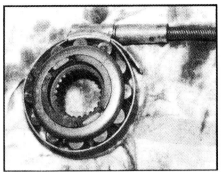

The next job was to reassemble the unidirectional clutch (59) – here the roller bearings are retained temporarily by a large jubilee clip to which a screwdriver is attached.

Then the unidirectional clutch is tapped into its housing in the centre of the annulus smooth side inwards (now check that it can revolve anticlockwise) followed by an oil thrower (57) which is held in place by a large circlip (58).

Next the two larger (72) of the two rear casing bearings was fitted, warming the case to aid fitting, followed by the fitting of the annulus (71).

Mr Tony Jeeves at GKN, 7 Cleveland Row, London SW1A 1DB). A good manual, or at least a clear exploded diagram, is a great asset not only in the workshop but also when explaining to your parts supplier which items are needed.

Reassembly

It is essential to ensure that all components are perfectly clean when reassembled and to use the minimum amount of oil needed for assembly purposes to minimise the risk of picking up dust, etc, which would 'stick' to the oil but not to the clean dry component. It is advisable not to use gasket sealing or joint-

This picture shows the annulus shaft protruding through the rear casing and the speedometer driving gear about to be fitted flange side inwards. This is followed by a plain spacer (73), a bearing (75), an oil seal (76), the flange (77) and a large washer and nut (78/9).

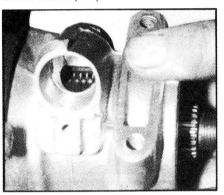

You can check the alignment of the speedo driving gear by peering through the housing for the speedo drive assembly as shown here.

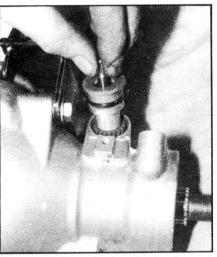

When a new 'O' ring has been fitted to the speedo drive assembly it can be fitted in its housing as shown in this picture . . .

. . . and secured by the fork which is bolted to the outside of the casing, (66, 67).

Here the sunwheel (53) is being inserted into the clutch sliding member (54). Note that on the splines which protrude slightly through the other side of the sunwheel there is a groove for a circlip – do not forget to fit this circlip.

Here the thrust ball race (16) is being fitted into the thrust ring (14) – make sure that the groove on the inner face of the thrust ring is clean and fit the retaining circlip (17).

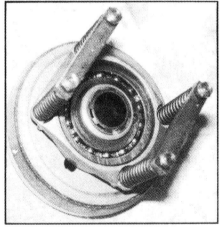

The thrust ring and bearing are then pressed on over the sunwheel and retained by another circlip.

ing compound when fitting overdrive gaskets as there is a risk that excess compound will become loose inside the overdrive and eventually block an oilway.

The reassembly work is covered in detail in the picture captions but there are one or two additional points that I would like to emphasise here. When the reassembled the unidirectional clutch (having taken note of its

Scimitar/Laycock Overdrive Rebuild

C O N T I N U E D

Back to the rear casing again and here the planet wheels and carrier (52) are being inserted . . .

. . . followed by the clutch sliding member (54) and the thrust ring assembly (14).

We have removed the nuts, bridge pieces and springs from the thrust pins and in this picture Eric is fitting the brake ring (11), to which the first gasket has been attached with a smear of grease. By fitting the first gasket to the brake ring (rather than to the casing) we avoided nicking the gasket with the sharp edge of the brake ring. The gasket on the side of the brake ring which is facing us in this picture is added next – again with a smear of grease to hold it in place. It is advisable not to use gasket seal on these gaskets.

New springs (13) are fitted to the thrust pins and the centre casing is put in position but will not go fully home against the brake ring at first . . .

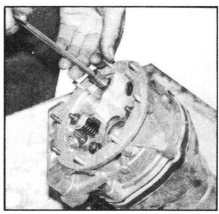

. . . so it is necessary to fit washers over the thrust pins and use the old shakeproof nuts to overcome the spring pressure . . .

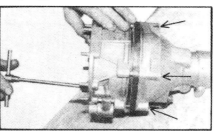

. . . and close up the casing until the external studs start to protrude as shown here (arrowed). Then the external washers and nuts can be fitted and when tight the old shakeproof nuts can be removed from the thrust pins again and the bridge pieces fitted using new shakeproof nuts (flat side towards bridge piece).

The next task is to fit new 'O' rings to the pistons (discard the old ones as they are removed so that they cannot be confused with the new ones) having first checked the pistons carefully for signs of wear or damage. Put clean oil into the cylinders then insert the pistons 'O' ring end first.

Now fit the lubrication relief valve ball, spring and plug as shown here

Here the new dashpot assembly (bought as a complete unit) fitted with new 'O' rings is about to be fitted into the housing directly below it. The blanking plug for the dashpot assembly is also fitted with a new 'O' ring.

The (50) cam is now fitted to the output shaft of the gearbox with woodruff key (51) and a circlip on either side to locate it – make sure the circlips fit properly into their grooves. The cam operates the overdrive oil pump via pump/plunger (39).

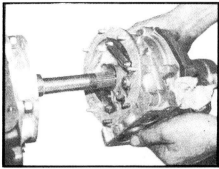

The front sections of the overdrive casing (adaptor plate) was fitted last month to retain the gearbox mainshaft but removed during this job whilst we fitted the cam and circlip to the shaft – now it can be refitted using its gaskets and jointing compound. At this stage we refitted the overdrive to the gearbox.

construction during dismantling) Eric used a jubilee clip to retain the roller bearings (see picture 4). When all the bearings were in place the clip was tightened in the manner of a piston ring compressor, that is, to a sufficient extent to enable the unidirectional clutch assembly to be gently tapped into its housing in the centre of the annulus leaving the jubilee clip behind.

This overdrive unit has not worked previously whilst in our ownership and several new parts were fitted during reassembly. The parts which should be renewed as a matter of course are 'O' rings, circlips, shakeproof nuts, and oil seals. The bearings in the rear casing were found to be in serviceable condition but other bearings were renewed. The springs on the thrust pins were also renewed and we noted that the old springs were a good ⅛″ shorter than the new ones.

Overdrives are expected to work equally well on a wide variety of vehicles whilst sharing the gearbox oil which will also vary from

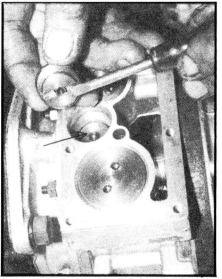

Next the non-return valve seat was fitted into sits housing (arrowed) with its ball bearing (33), followed by the pump plug which contains the non-return spring (32) to which Eric is pointing with the screwdriver.

Now fit the gasket where the bottom cover will fit to the overdrive. The blanking plug (10) which Eric is holding is about to be screwed into the pressure tapping point (this is where overdrive testing equipment is connected). Note that the three large plugs shown in this picture are (from right to left) the dashpot plug (24), the pump plug (31), and the pressure filter plug (37).

Now the filter can be fitted – it has a locating device in the centre of its opposite side which locates in the hole shown in the previous picture – and this is followed by the cover plate.

The assembly is completed by fitting the new solenoid as shown here (83).

one manufacturer to another. The important points to remember are that regardless of the type of oil used it must be perfectly clean, and no-anti-friction additives should be used. □

NEXT MONTH
The Scimitar's front suspension and steering overhaul.

"Christmas wouldn't be Christmas without the lucky valve spring in his pud . . ."

"And of course, we musn't forget to leave something out for Father Christmas must we?"

Reliant Scimitar
Part Five

Overhauling the TR4/5/6 type front suspension – our Scimitar GTE demonstrates the problems. By John Williams.

Many cars have independent front suspension by coil springs and wishbones and the lessons to be learnt by overhauling the front suspension on our Reliant Scimitar GTE will therefore have numerous applications.

We have intended to report on the overhaul of the steering components but while Eric Gilbert was dismantling the suspension he examined the steering rack and linkages and found them to be in good order; so unlike our major restoration projects, the Scimitar (which is supposed to be 'Rolling Rebuild') will not be receiving attention to every single

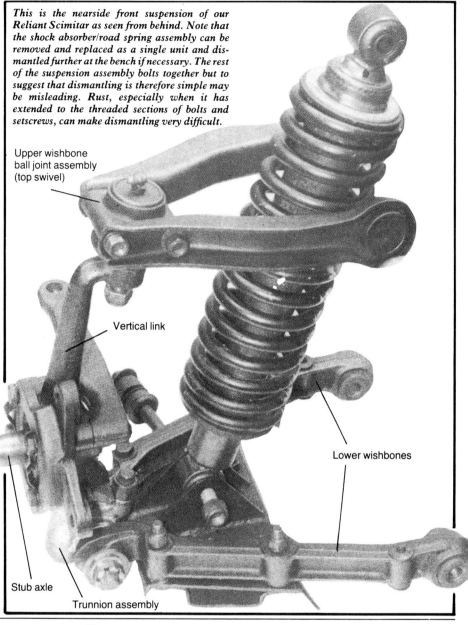

This is the nearside front suspension of our Reliant Scimitar as seen from behind. Note that the shock absorber/road spring assembly can be removed and replaced as a single unit and dismantled further at the bench if necessary. The rest of the suspension assembly bolts together but to suggest that dismantling is therefore simple may be misleading. Rust, especially when it has extended to the threaded sections of bolts and setscrews, can make dismantling very difficult.

Upper wishbone ball joint assembly (top swivel)

Vertical link

Lower wishbones

Stub axle

Trunnion assembly

Scimitar Suspension Overhaul

area. Eric, by the way is an independent motor engineer based in Beckenham (telephone 01-650 1342) who has become such an enthusiastic member of the *Practical Classics* team – doing almost everything except the

actual typing and photography – that I sometimes wonder whether he is after my job!

It is easy to say "dismantle the suspension", and with or without a workshop manual the theory is fairly simple. There will almost certainly be problems with stubborn nuts and bolts and the liberal use of penetrating fluid at least a few hours before work commences will certainly help. If more extreme measures are needed, and especially if you are contemplating using heat, be sure to consult an expert first so as to avoid weakening components treated in this way.

Scimitar Suspension Overhaul

C O N T I N U E D

When the overhaul work entails removing the calipers from the car, that is, disconnecting the hydraulic system it is a good idea to ensure that the caliper pots (or pistons) are driven out of their housings far enough to enable them to be removed later. Once the hydraulic system has been disconnected pots which are inaccessible may be driven out by using compressed air but only if ALL the pistons (three in this instance) are still in their housings.

Our Scimitar is fitted with brake pads which are wired so that when the lining is partly worn an electrical circuit is completed between the wire (embedded in the lining) and the brake disc and this activates a warning light on the dashboard.

An advantage of the Scimitars suspension is that the road springs are loaded against the shock absorbers and each spring and shock absorber can be removed from the car as a single unit. Therefore, unless you need to

This view of the old brake discs tells more about the extent of the rust than the degree of real wear that has taken place, especially as there are no "ridges" marking the edges of the lining contact area.

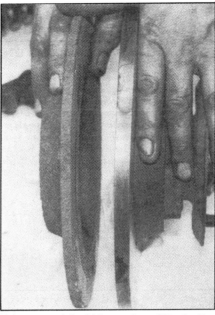

Eric measured the thickness of our old brake discs and concluded that they must have been excessively skimmed at some time because they were well below the minimum thickness (which is stated on new discs) of 0.450" but there was no "wear ridge". The difference in thickness between old and new discs can be clearly seen in this picture.

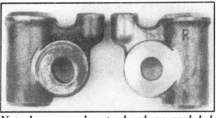

Note how wear has produced an oval hole through the old bottom trunnion on the left.

separate them you can avoid the potentially dangerous task of unloading the springs. If you do need to separate the springs from the shock absorbers this can be done at the bench but be sure to use spring compressors which are adequate for the job – you may have to hire compressors if your own are not long enough for the Scimitars springs. Take precautions to ensure that if an accident occurs and a spring 'escapes' it will do the minimum of damage.

Having dismantled the suspension Eric cleaned and examined everything and all wearing parts were renewed with the exception of the upper wishbone ball joints (top

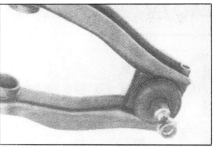

The upper ball joints were found to be in serviceable condition – if worn they would be obviously loose, in which case they would be discarded and new ball joints fitted.

Note the positions of the Allen headed screws through the outer ends of the upper wishbone – the wishbones should be fitted so that the holes for the outer screws are higher than the inner ones.

swivels). All the new parts were supplied promptly by Queensberry Road Garage (0536 513351). It is worth noting that unlike many other cars with similar front suspension assemblies the Scimitar did not have shims in the top swivel assembly for altering the castor angle, and none were shown in the workshop manual.

Our new springs and shock absorbers were supplied as separate components and, as dif-

This picture shows the thick bolt which passes through the lower wishbones and the trunnion complete with the small components which fit within and alongside the wishbone – the same components are shown separately below and they are (from the edges of the picture to the centre) a pair of stout steel washers, a pair of nylon or plastic bushes, a pair of 'O' rings which fit in the pair of cupped washers, and a single steel sleeve. When dismantling these parts take note of the order in which they are fitted and which way round the cupped washers and 'O' rings are facing.

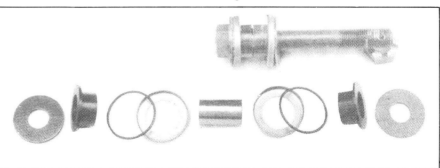

This close-up picture of the trunnion/lower wishbone assembly shows that the cupped washers face away from the wishbones arms. Don't forget to replace the steering lock stop which screws into the housing (arrowed).

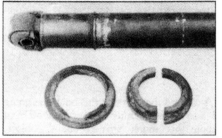

On the left is the spring retaining ring with a pair of collets on the right.

Only one collet is shown here to illustrate how the collets seat against the ridge on the lower end of the shock absorber housing thus providing a seating for the spring retaining ring – of course the shock absorber passes through the centre of the spring.

ferent shock absorbers tend to require different ancillary equipment in order to accommodate the road springs, it is important to keep the old units as some items may have to be transferred to the new. For example, at the upper end of our shock absorbers the spring retaining ring rested against a substantial flange which was part of the shock absorber body. On the new units a narrow ridge around the shock absorber body accommodates a stout ring (like a large flat washer) which was supplied with the shock absorber. This combination of the narrow ridge and the stout ring took the place of the substantial flange of the old shock absorber and it was against this that the spring retaining ring (transferred from the old shock absorber) seated. The arrangement employed at the lower end of the shock absorber is shown in the pictures.

It is useful to employ a method of marking components which will neither interfere with nor be obliterated by cleaning. Eric 'marks' all components from the right-hand side of the car by twisting a short length of thin wire around each of them; components from the left-hand side of the car remain unmarked.

The top inner wishbone mounting bracket remained attached to the car. There are shims behind this bracket to determine the camber angle and, so far, we have seen no reason to disturb the bracket. Each end of the top inner wishbone spindle passes through two half bushes (rubber) which are housed in the top bracket. The spindle should be examined to see whether it has become corroded under the rubber bushes – if so it should be replaced (or the corrosion removed and the surface of the spindle restored) – this corrosion would greatly shorten the life of new bushes.

Although there may be a little movement between the vertical link and the trunnion when they are off the car but screwed together, when fully assembled on the car and greased, this movement will disappear. The outer lower wishbone spindle nuts can be tightened up when assembled to 50-65 lbs/ft, the inner wishbone mountings (top and bottom) should be tightened up by hand until they are obviously as tight as they can be (they cannot be overtightened) but it is important that the inner wishbone mountings – and preferably the outer ones too – are not finally tightened until the car, complete with engine, has been put back on its wheels so that the suspension can find its natural level.

The installation of wheel bearings requires some care. In order to ensure that wheel bearings seat correctly the stub axle nut should be tightened up gradually, but with the road wheel fitted and spinning, to 35 lbs/ft. It is essential to spin the wheel whilst tightening this nut, failure to do so can result in damage to the bearings. Having reached this torque

...and were allowing the lower part of the old shock absorbers to bear against the brackets on the lower wishbone assembly.

Compared with the previous picture, this illustrates the correct clearance between the body of a new shock absorber and the bracket already mentioned.

figure, undo the nut two 'flats' and feel for vertical rocking movement at the road wheel (one hand at the top of the wheel, the other at the bottom) which should be present but very slight. Tighten the nut to reduce the vertical movement as much as possible without actually eliminating it altogether and the job is done.

Do not overgrease the wheel bearings. It is not necessary to pack in as much grease as can be made to go in, including filling the small hubcaps, indeed it is wrong to do so as excess grease will soon find its way out, probably fouling the brake discs, and certainly forcing the seal.

NEXT MONTH
We look at the rear suspension and the brake calipers.

Reliant Scimitar
Part Six

The rebuild nears completion — John Williams reports.

We have decided to hasten the completion of our Reliant Scimitar rebuild for two reasons; firstly we need to put the car on the road, secondly, the remaining work required by the car and on which I could usefully report to you has been found to be very little.

So, although I had expected to complete the overhaul work on the suspension and brakes this month, in fact I will complete the whole mechanical rebuild — that is, as much as we will be doing for the time being.

Brake Calipers

We decided to dismantle the brake calipers in order to examine the cylinders and pots for wear or damage, but they were found to be in

Brakes and Rear Suspension

good condition. Remember to use the brake hydraulics to drive the pots part of the way out of the cylinders before disconnecting the hydaulic pipes from the calipers. With the caliper at the bench the pots can then be removed by hand. Beware of hydraulic fluid at this stage, it tends to fly about as pots and seals

(Above)
At last the engine and gearbox are back in the Scimitar. Here Eric Gilbert manoevres the hoist complete with engine into position from which it was lowered very slowly, with both of us guiding it and keeping stray wires out of the way, onto its mountings where we continued to support it with the hoist until the gearbox was attached from beneath.

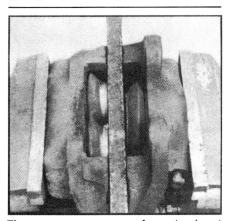

There are two ways to remove the pots (or pistons) from the calipers; they can be driven part of the way out of the cylinders by hydraulic pressure with the brake discs in place and before the hydraulic pipes are disconnected. Or the calipers can be removed from the car and the pots driven out by compressed air using a bar as shown here to ensure that none of the pots escapes from its cylinder before all have emerged far enough to be accessible for removal by hand later.

Dust covers, pots and rubber seals are removed from each caliper by hand. Note the grooves in the cylinder walls, these house the rubber seals and must be cleaned out thoroughly before new seals are fitted.

are removed and it is not good for paintwork or clothing. Remove the old rubber dust covers and the seals – the latter are like square section 'O' rings which fit into grooves around the cylinders. Use generous quantities of clean brake fluid to clean the calipers and pots, paying special attention to the grooves which accomodate the dust cover and seals.

More clean brake fluid should be used when reassembling, and note that one of the dust covers is in the shape of a figure '8', to fit both of the smaller cylinders. This cover is very difficult to fit and requires plenty of patience.

Drum brakes

Removal of the rear brake drums showed that the interiors of the drums were very dirty and looked as if there had been a long term (albeit slight) hydraulic fluid leak. The wheel cylinders should have been capable of sliding in slots in the brake back plates but they were seized. Existing components were cleaned and

The rear brakes were found to be worn, very dirty, and with wheel cylinders seized to the back plates. They were cleaned and new shoes and wheel cylinders fitted.

new wheel cylinders and brake shoes fitted. Eric Gilbert also decided to remove, clean, lubricate, and then replace the handbrake cable.

Rear suspension

The rear suspension required little attention. Apart from the shock absorbers, which appeared to be relatively new, it consists of two pairs of radius arms locating the axle fore and

For a car which weighs around 1 ton the Scimitar has a remarkably stout chassis. Here the cantilever arm and the transverse radius arms which centralise the rear axle can be seen. It is a pity that the differential drain plug is hidden behind the right-hand radius arm.

Here you can see the nearside pair of radius arms which are attached via large rubber bushes to the chassis and to the axle. There was little evidence of wear and no rear suspension bushes needed changing.

One small problem which has yet to be dealt with (at the time of writing) concerns the outriggers above the rear wheels both of which are thoroughly rusted

aft and a pair of transverse radius arms which keep the axle in a central position as it rises and falls in relation to the chassis. The fore and aft radius arms are attached to the chassis at their forward ends via large bushes and via similar bushes to the axle at their rear ends. Each transverse radius arm is attached via a bush to the chassis at its outer end and via another bush to a cantilever arm mounted (again via a large bush) to the rear of the differential casing.

Electrical and miscellaneous

The engine and gearbox (with overdrive) have been put back in the car. An engine hoist was used to drop the gearbox through the engine compartment onto boards over Eric Gilberts pit. The engine was then dropped in separately, and slowly lowered onto its mountings whilst Eric and I guided it and kept various wires out of the way of the manifolds. Then the gearbox was manoevred into position on a trolley jack.

The wiring in this car is in fair condition, but Eric has decided to check it all for corrosion, brittle insulation, etc, and to clean all connectors. Several wires will be shortened when brittle or corroded sections are cut out or corroded connectors removed and new ones fitted but this is not expected to create difficulties and there is certainly not enough bad wiring to justify the trouble and expense of obtaining and fitting a new loom.

As regards the interior, the seat frames were repaired by Beaufort Restorations at Maidstone some months ago, but the dashboard will require some attention in order to make the instruments and switches more secure.

Repairs to the inner nearside front wing and battery box area were carried out by the Lenham Motor Company in May this year. Generally the bodywork is sound, but there is a certain amount of crazing on the surface of the glass fibre, and the paintwork is becoming a little flat.

We will be treating this car to further bodywork renovation in a few months time followed

...rather than in its previous position below the fuel pump as shown here – fuel pumps and electrical equipment should be kept apart to avoid unnecessary fire hazards.

The engine was refitted complete with manifolds as shown here. The manifolds are easier to fit before the engine goes back in the car but it does mean that extra care is needed in guiding the engine into position. The reconditioned radiator was fitted later.

The wiring and electrical connectors required a certain amount of restoration but as the main electrical feed comes via the starter motor, circuit testing could not commence until the starter motor was back in place. Eric has decided to reposition the coil behind the windscreen wiper motor on the nearside bulkhead...

by a respray. Meanwhile it will be put back on the road as a staff car, and a very sound car at that, for Michael Brisby (our former editor who now edits 'The Automobile') and he will no doubt report upon his impressions of the car from time to time in Staff Car Sagas.

Finally, I must pay tribute to Queensberry Road Garage (28-32 Queensberry Road, Kettering, Northants, telephone Kettering 513351) the Scimitar specialists who have dealt patiently with all of our enquiries concerning parts and have made Erics task much easier by ensuring that parts were delivered very quickly, often within hours of being ordered. □

USING GLASS FIBRE

In this, the first of four articles about GRP, we shall be looking at the basic equipment, materials, and the safety aspects. The following articles will cover causes of gel cracking and accident damage, repairs and, finally, stripping and preparing GRP bodies for painting.

So, having acquired your GRP-bodied dream car all smothered in cracks and accident damage, you have to understand what glassfibre is all about and how to go about repairing it. The most important thing to realise is that it takes an awful lot of time and you can't skimp on anything, otherwise the final repairs will look like the surface of the moon. All repair techiques are the same whether you're working on a Reliant Robin or a GT40, and why some professionals charge an arm and a leg for repairing a high-class GRP car is beyond me because it takes the same amount of time to repair a crack on a Reliant Robin as it does on a 308 GTB Ferrari.

Materials

Starting right at the beginning for this series of articles I shall list only what you really need.

MAT – this is strands of silicon (glass) chopped and laid down in varying densities and chemically dressed for ease of handling. Unless you are using it for large sheet areas use only 300gm/m (the old 1oz/yd) as it bends around corners easily.

TISSUE – a very fine mat looking like a Kleenex tissue to cover gel cracks etc. It gives a very fine finished surface. There are only two mats used, although there are glassfibre tapes and heavy mats known as woven rovings where hanks of glassfibre are woven together to give a heavy drape.

RESIN – this is the other half of the GRP (glass reinforced plastic) and is clear polyester resin. In fact resin is solid, but it is dissolved in a solvent called styrene which gives it its characteristic smell.

GEL COAT RESIN – used in moulds, it is a thixotropic polyester resin, much thicker than the ordinary lay-up resin above and will not run on vertical surfaces.

HARDENER – when you buy your resin you will automatically be given hardener either in paste or liquid form. It is actually methy ethyl ketone peroxide (MEK or MEKP for short).

ACETONE – is the brush or roller cleaner and this is the only solvent. You cannot use detergent and hot water. If the brushes go solid then you throw them away. With brushes always buy the correct resin type as they are cheap and contain fewer bristles than ordinary paint brushes; this allows the acetone to get in between the bristles and clean them thoroughly. Normal paint brushes will end up stiff in some places and become effectively useless.

Two other products which are essential are the chopped strand glass paste (Davids P40) which is as it says, a paste which when mixed with hardener will form a very strong bond and filler found on just about every car known to man, be it metal or GRP. Filler is chalk dust in resin and, when mixed with

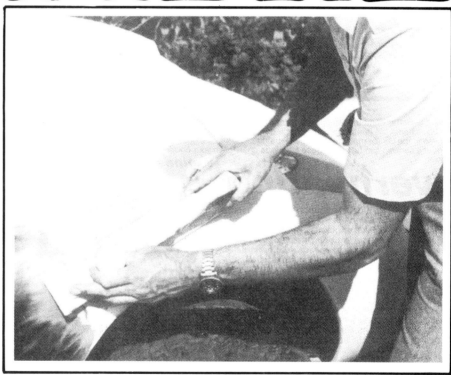

Part 1: Materials, equipment and safety, by Miles Wilkins.

Experienced DIY enthusiasts will be aware that the right tools contribute so much to the ease and success of any job and tools and materials are the main theme of this introduction to working with glassfibre. This picture shows the 3M file in use and it is available from motor factors.

hardener, forms a spreadable paste which can cover a multitude of sins but, in our case of course, produces the perfect repair. Fillers come in all shapes and sizes but we used Davids P38 or Upol C. With all purchases buy the largest quantity you want, ie. do not buy silly tubes of Plastic Padding to do a whole car as it is a gross waste of money. With

fillers buy from a motor factor in 4kg tins or so. That way you get trade, the 500gm tin in the local accessory shop costing just about the same as the 4kg tin from a factor!

Resins – again buy in 5 litre (10kg) tins along with your brushes, acetone and mat (sold by the metre). Strand Glassfibre Ltd, Brentway Trading Estate, Brentford,

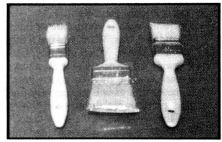

A selection of 1in, 1½in, and 2in resin brushes.

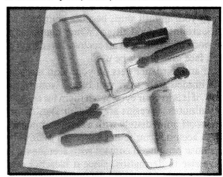

A selection of rollers for use on very large flat areas where it is quicker to use rollers than brushes.

P38/Upol C filler and the chopped strand mat P40. The Upol C is 7kg size but either 2.5 or 4kg will be ideal for normal purposes.

Middx. TW8 8ER (telephone: 01 568 7191), are the only retail outlet in the UK and are helpful; if you have access to a trade outlet (where I buy my stuff) it will be even less again. Failing that, yacht chandlers will provide resins etc., although buying this way is unbelievably expensive. So, to recap so far, the materials needed are mat, tissue, resin, brushes (and rollers) and acetone.

Tools

Now the basic tools with which to attack the damage. A hacksaw, chisels, Stanley knife, plenty of tins and sticks to mix up the resin (NEVER use a glass container as the heat of reaction between resin and hardener when it goes off will shatter the glass), a jig saw and a Grinderette – either Wolf or Bosch. They really are essential for preparing gel cracks etc. They are expensive to buy outright but,

A complete range of tools to cover every eventuality.

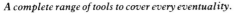

300 gm/m (1oz) mat alongside the fine tissue.

if tackling a whole car, then it is worth it; failing that, hire one. If desperate, you can use an electric drill with either a cintride disc on it or an adhesive disc on a backing pad.

You'll also need plenty of sandpapers in varying grades and a selection of cork, rubber blocks and the specialist files (as in the photograph) made by 3M available from motor factors – their sanding files are invaluable. Recapping again; for cutting the mat – Stanley knife and scissors. For preparing the body – Grinderette, hacksaw (padsaw), jig saw for cutting and trimming, sandpapers. For finishing – files, rasp files, blocks and sandpapers; both production paper, ie. carborundum chips glued on a backing paper used dry, going from P40 coarse to P800 fine, and wet and dry silica chips glued on a waterproof backing paper used either wet or dry going from 40 to 1500 which is just like newspaper. A usual selection is P40 and P80 for rubbing down filler and 360, 600 wet and dry for final finishing prior to painting.

All your equipment will last indefinitely, the only exceptions being the resin and fillers which have a shelf life of around nine months. In other words, they may 'go off' after this time. In reality, however, resins will last at least two years and so will fillers if the lids are tightly on them and they are left away from sunlight in a cool place. When a crust starts to form then it's time to throw them away. Acetone lasts indefinitely. All this will be useless if, of course, you are allergic to resins or mat, and I suppose I should

A Wolf Grinderette with a cutting disc on it and, separately, the sanding disc – this is 80 grade.

The specialist 3M Stickit file with its adhesive sandpaper strips. Cork and rubber blocks are also essential.

have started this article with some notes about health and safety.

Health precautions

You are likely to get a localised rash up your arms and hands if you handle the mat with no precautions. If you are allergic, *do not continue*. Get someone else to do the job as the allergy can cause severe swelling, rashes and can be extremely painful. Cover up your arms when cutting or handling mat and use washing-up gloves of necessary. If, like me, you cannot stand gloves then always use a barrier cream which is available from Boots, most chemists, resin shops, etc. Resins normally give people no problems, apart from the smell which may upset you. Always give yourself good ventilation when doing a job since the heavy vapour given off (styrene) can cause headaches and even unconsciousness if you are exposed to it for too long. If you ever feel drowsiness coming on get out

immediately into the fresh air.

The warning signs for resins are an itchy nose and running eyes. When you reach this stage *stop and recover*. When grinding, cutting or sawing a laminate you must always wear a mask and goggles and always grind outside, never in a garage etc., as very fine pure glass particles are thrown everywhere and once they are inhaled the body doesn't get rid of them. Silicosis can result (and this is similar to asbestosis). For the one-off job a simple face mask is enough provided you keep your mouth shut, because your nose is an extremely good filter. When doing long periods of grinding in an enclosed area then a full face mask must be used.

If any hardener gets on your skin wash it off immediately as it will bleach your skin and, if it is in your eyes, wash them for at least 10 minutes. If resins are on your skin, wipe them off immediately with a cloth dampened with acetone (you're not supposed to do this because prolonged contact with acetone may give rise to dermatitis, since it bleaches out the natural skin oils), then wash in warm soapy water and finally rub a skin cream over the affected part (Nivea is very good). If any is swallowed, drink quantities of water and induce vomiting – *seek medical aid immediately*.

If any hardener spills on the ground or clothing, wash it away with plenty of water. With resins cover with earth or sand and, when soaked in, dispose of safely; wipe the residue off the ground with acetone.

Safety during work

Fire is a major hazard. All resins, hardeners, and acetone are extremely inflammable. All have low flash points, ie. temperatures at which they may ignite; resin is 25-30 deg. C. So *do not* use naked lights and *do not* smoke while doing a job or even when you've finished because the styrene vapour given off

USING GLASS FIBRE

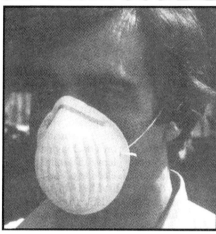

A simple but effective face mask made by 3M and available from motor factors. Alternatively, the Martingale face mask consisting of a renewable cotton pad held in by a metal frame is available from Boots or from resin shops.

during curing is highly volatile. Once cured, though, it takes a lot of heat to make GRP burn.

Fire can also be started by throwing away your unused liquid resin in the dustbin because the heat of reaction when it is setting is enough to set alight any paper. Always place the tin in a safe place and wait until it

has 'gone off' and is **stone cold** before you dispose of it. If a fire starts, a CO2 or dry powder extinguisher will cover all possibilities. Always keep an extinguisher handy. Water will not work on resins. All resins that you buy are known as pre-accelerated resins and all you do is add hardener. However, without trying to confuse the issue, unaccelerated resins are available for operatives to add their own accelerator (cobalt napthalate) to give predetermined set times. If anyone offers you unaccelerated resin do not use it. Buy the correct accelerated type. Accelerator is always added first to the resin, then the hardener. **Never** mix accelerator and hardener together because they form an **explosive mixture.**

Unaccelerated resins are usually not available over the counter and, unless specifically asked for, all resins sold are already pre-accelerated so don't worry. Working with GRP is commonsense. Treat all chemic ls with the respect they deserve and, if you're allergic, STOP.

Glossary

Finally, for this month here are some terms as used in GRP with which most of us are familiar. The process of GRP is called *laying up*, brushing or rolling resin through the mat is known as *wetting out* and the finished solid is the *laminate*. When 'going off' it is known as *curing* and, just before it is set solid, the laminate is at the *green stage*. With moulds and moulding the untrimmed article is known as the *rough moulding*, and two other terms are *release wax* or *release agent* which provide the barrier between mould and article for release purposes. □

NEXT MONTH
Stress cracks and how to avoid them

"I bet Granny's glad you bought a four-seater classic, dear".

USING GLASS FIBRE

Every GRP car on the road today has a gel crack on it or at least a blemish in the GRP paintwork. Even the best prepared car at a concours event, or or brand new car even, will have a mark somewhere if you look close enough! Gel cracks are really GRP's answer to metal rust and, like rust, most of them should never appear. So, apart from the obvious accident damage (about which more later) how do gel cracks appear, and why, and what can be done to prevent them from happening in the first place?

Starting at the beginning, causes are from the mould itself. If the mould has been constructed from GRP (be it epoxy or polyester resin) and has an inbuilt crack in it or any other blemishes, then the pattern of the crack will be transferred to the moulding and will show as 'crack indentation'. This is fairly common on, dare I say it, low budget kit cars and on cheap replacement wings, bonnets etc. for Morris Minors and the like. At least with the replacement parts the offending mark can be flatted off with wet and dry paper and then the whole panel primed and painted but, with self-coloured panels (where the colour is in the gel coat layer), then the blemish is there for all to see and if it is on, say, a flat bonnet area it will stick out like a sore thumb, much to the detriment of your pristine car. The only recourse is to paint out the fault and get the manufacturer to rectify the mould and make another one. (The classic example, as reported to me when I admonished one poor kit car manufacturer about the shocking state of a door panel was 'Oh, they're all like that'!).

From the mould itself we move on to the next stage where the moulding is released from the mould. If, for any reason, the moulding has not fully cured (ie. it is still green), or has stuck fast because the release agent failed to release and too much force is applied, stress lines and cracks will appear and will show up as white lines. Then, if left unchecked, they immediately show through the paint that is applied subsequently. The remedy here is to make sure all the release agent is evently applied — especially into any awkward corners — and that the moulding

A rather extreme form of damage illustrating GRP's ability to absorb the impact and then shatter, restricting the area of major damage.

Part 2: Miles Wilkins explains the causes of GRP damage and how to prevent it.

has fully cured before attempting to release it. It may also be that the mould design itself has been constructed in the wrong way to allow an easy release from the moulding ie. too sharp a radius on corners, overhanging angles, double curvatures, etc. If necessary a re-design must be done to prevent inherent cracks in the moulding.

With a crack-free moulding released, inbuilt stresses may eventually appear as a crack, especially on hard butt edges where not enough thickness has been applied. Unless bonded to GRP correctly different materials, such as plywood or steel bul-

kheads, can move, causing stresses on the GRP. A thick laminate joining a thin flexible panel or a door panel beefed up around a hinge point will cause a gel crack to appear in time where the thin panel flexes and the stiffer hinge panel doesn't. The remedy on any panel is to grade the weight of mat accordingly, rising evenly to a maximum around the stress point. Sadly, too many new GRP car

manufacturers don't even bother and the factory laminators just slop it on any old way. If the cars were built correctly then they would be virtually bomb-proof and, having repaired just about every type of GRP car, I feel that so much could be done to prevent totally unnecessary damage.

Moving to the vehicle itself, what can be done to prevent cracks? The main problems

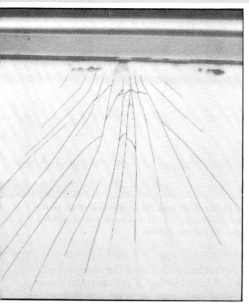

Extent of gel crazing as a result of movement from a window frame.

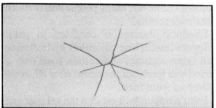

Gel crack from a stone chip from the underside of a wheel arch which has "penetrated" the panel. This should be dealt with without delay while the damaged area is comparatively small.

Cracking around a door handle due to excessive stress.

the panel. A correctly fitting panel will require no force to shut or open it but force, wherever it is applied, will lead to cracks. NEVER slam doors and lids because cracks will appear in time.

With bulkheads and glass windscreens, build up the area around the aperture to prevent flexing if required, but grade it away to the original thickness otherwise it will crack somewhere else.

Fitting trim and badges on a newly painted body is another cause of cracks and heart-ache. Drill the rivet or screw hole OVER-SIZE ie. if using ⅛in rivets use a %4in drill; do NOT force in a rivet or screw because as soon as you tighten up — bang — a star crack will appear through the paint around the fixing. If possible always use a washer behind the rivet or screw to spread the load. With badges use double sided adhesive tape if possible to save using screws or rivets. Remember, any mark will remain for life and may spread. The only way to get rid of it is to do a repair and repaint. Fitting the 'pretty' bits causes more damage to new GRP bodies than any other operation.

Other areas to watch are the fitting of non-standard items like sun roofs, fancy air cleaners etc. and not realising that they are chaffing on the adjacent GRP panels, thus causing damage. With any item do not force a panel over it; always check first that it does not foul before shutting the panel. With any exhaust system, wiring and water pipes make sure there is a large enough hole or air space around the pipes so they don't touch and

Furthermore, pulling out metal bodywork, aligning on jigs and welding on new panels actually puts more stress into the bodyshell, whereas bonding on a new GRP panel should cause NO stress at all.

After a major accident the extent of gel crazing may not be evident until some days or even weeks later, when it shows. Driving a car after a minor accident will cause the cracking to spread, making life difficult for any accident estimator to assess the TRUE damage. I always look for the slight deflections of light over the paintwork to tell me where the cracking stops, even though nobody else can even see the cracks underneath the paint. It goes without saying that all the accident damage/crazing must be removed completely to prevent any further stress/gel cracks occurring again on the 're-paired' area. All too often new sections are

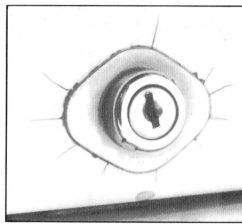

Cracks due to stress around the lock.

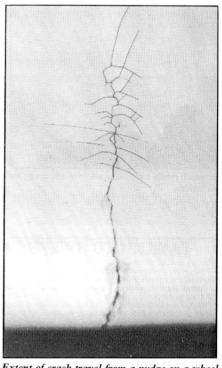

Extent of crack travel from a nudge on a wheel arch.

are due to high stress points ie. door hand-les, hinges etc. and panel flexing due to a stiff bulkhead flexing the panel around it. This also applies to glass windscreens, be it front or rear, where the glass is heavy and does not give — but the GRP panel will. All fittings on any panel must have the load spread over as large an area as possible, especially around the door and boot handles. If necessary, add one or two extra laminates behind the handle and grade them over an area, then use large 'penny' washers when bolting up. With all fittings DO NOT bolt up like a gorilla. Use commonsense otherwise that sickening cracking sound will be heard and, yes, there is a crack on your brand new paint. Make sure with any panel that it fits correctly ie. all doors, bonnets and boot lids fit their shut lines, since tugging away on the handle trying to open the door will only succeed in cracking

cause cracks. With any wiring always use a rubber grommet to prevent the raw edge cutting into the wires. Make sure underpanels, such as wheel arches, are well protected by anti-stone chip paint (3M supply a good one) or a good FLEXIBLE underbody seal so stones flung up by the wheel do not star crack the GRP from underneath (Lotus Elans and Europas suffer from this).

Most, if not all, of the foregoing can usually be avoided with simple precautions and attention to detail. The next cause cannot! It is that of accident damage. Proper GRP cars (such as Reliant, Lotus, TVR and Marcos) are infinitely better in an accident than metal cars because GRP will absorb the impact and shatter, NOT deform, thus minimising panel damage. Metal will deform and go on deform-ing ie. a front panel through the wing, a post, roof, door etc. and be a total write-off.

bonded in and 6in behind the joint all that is under the new paint are the remains of gel craz-ing from the accident. If new sections are bonded in it is essential that the thickness of

USING GLASS FIBRE

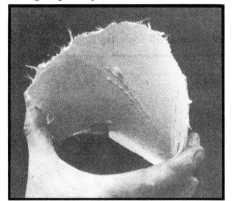

Fire damage. Note how the resin has burned leaving the powdery mat.

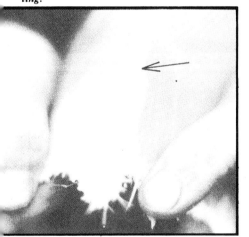

Overflexing will cause cracks and paint splitting.

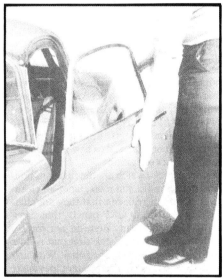

How to shut a door properly with a hand flat against the panel to spread the minimum force necessary over as large an area as possible.

Part of an Elan boot lid after an accident showing extensive gel cracks and paint peeling off between the gel crack lines.

the new laminate matches the old and the join itself must be graded over a wide area.

Other causes of GRP damage, apart from fire which we touched on last month, are confined to nature. GRP will delaminate if left out for years with no protection; water will enter the mat strands which act like capillaries and, if there is a severe frost, the layers can physically separate. Once water is in GRP then it must be dried out in an oven for about a week at 85-100 deg. F before any attempt at repairs or painting can take place otherwise water will just break through, giving unsightly bubbles and blisters on the paint surface.

Severe heat will distort the panel or bodyshell. Above 140 deg. F the resin MAY start to 'flow' and, once set again, the deformed panel will have to be replaced. This is why one NEVER low bakes GRP bodies when painting (however, many people still try with disastrous results).

Chemical damage is confined to paint strippers (methylene chloride), hydroflouric acid (glass etching) and certain fuels over a period will leech out the resin (after all, resin is derived from fuel).

Paint strippers will eat into the gel coat and resin and, if left, will make a hole. The only action is to cut out and repair. Hydroflouric acid not only will eat into the GRP but will eat into you as well! HF is NOT available to the public due to its lethal qualities. Brake fluids and anti-freezes do not attack GRP. Fire is the most feared and any fire damage on GRP MUST be cut away since only the glass mat is left. The mat has no strength at all after the resin has burnt away. Never bond new panels to fire-damaged old ones because, at best, you will make a very weak bond.

GRP is pretty indestructible and really will last a lifetime if looked after correctly.

> **NEXT MONTH**
> Crack repair and bonding
> on a new section.

"This isn't quite what I imagined when you said you'd inherited a large estate in the country"

This part is really the nub of the matter — how to repair your crazed dream car. The repairs can be divided into three types. (1) simple gel cracks, (2) compound accident/gel crack damage requiring reinforcement and, (3) major accident damage requiring replacement sections.

The simple gel crack

The first thing to realise is that *every* GRP car will have a gel crack on it somewhere. Even brand new cars will or, after a professional respray, a crack will appear from just knocking it in the garage or by fixing new items of trim, badges, etc., so don't get paranoid about gel cracks. They may look unsightly and annoying but, unlike rust on metal cars, they are not going to affect the structure in any way. I have just supplied a brand new Esprit Turbo hot off the transporter with two gel cracks on it due to over-zealous trim fitting but fortunately they didn't show! The worst thing to do is to eliminate just one crack and make more of a mess doing so; it is far better to save up and do the whole car in one go, culminating in a superb respray. The second thing to understand is that it TAKES TIME, a great deal of time, to carry out repairs correctly and, as described in the

On large areas pre-resin and drape one piece of tissue all over the repair, using two layers if necessary. ▶

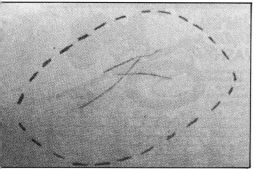

A gel crack! Dotted line indicates the extent of the area which needs grinding.

opening article of this series, the technique is the same for ANY GRP car. The cost of professionally repairing a Reliant or Ferrari is equal and only the final painting and finish will give the price differential.

With the simple crack then, wash the car first. It is amazing how many people gaily grind away, sweeping all the muck into the freshly ground area and then splodging over the mess with filler. Dry it thoroughly and de-wax the area if required with white spirit or 2-star fuel. Now comes the moment of truth. Get your grinderette and remove the guard so you can obtain the correct FLAT angle of attack and gently grind the crack area, overlapping the end of each crack line by at least an inch. The crack shows up as a dark yellow line so you know when it stops. DO NOT graunch away at such an angle that you go straight through the lot but use just a gentle angle ie. 15 degrees to the horizontal. DO NOT (as, incredibly, many manuals tell you)

USING GLASS FIBRE

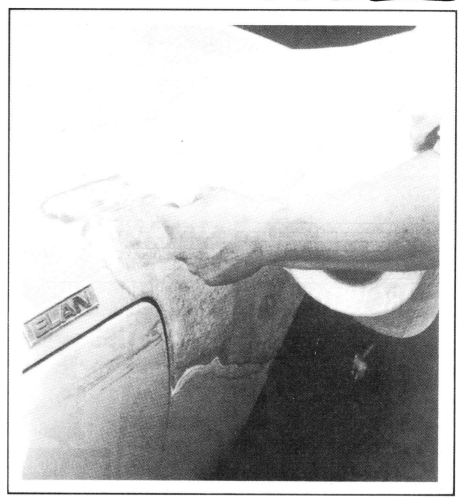

PART 3: This month Miles Wilkins guides us through repair techniques from a gel crack to major accident damage.

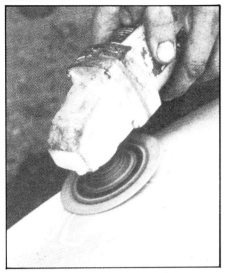

Grinding out the crack. Note the flat angle of attack of the grinderette. 80 grade paper is used.

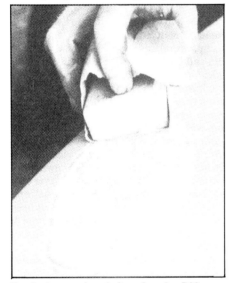

Feathering out the grind marks using P80 paper on a cork block.

ROUT OUT each line of the crack and fill it with filler, rather like doing lino-cuts at school (do they still do lino-cuts?) because each 'line' will show as soon as it is painted. Grind enough away to just enter the mat layer, ie. go through the paint and gel coat layer. The mat layer will show up white and 'rough hairy' to the touch. Use an 80 grade paper disc on the grinderette. Next feather the paint/grind edge with 80 production paper at 90 degrees to the grind mark to remove the marks and to give a gentle slope to the repair. Another myth — there is no such thing as re-gelling. You do not put gel coat resin over the area because gel resin is sticky on the top surface and you cannot rub it down but, more to the point, any resin on its own is brittle and the crack will work through again. In the same vein, filler alone will have the same effect but 90% of so called repair specialists will just grind away and slop filler over it and in about four to six weeks the marks will show through the paint again. The next stage is the only correct way and that is to paint resin over the ground area and 'lay up' the piece of tissue which has been pre-cut to shape. Just jiggle the resin up to the

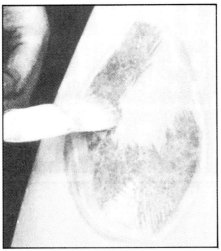

Area is now ready for repair and the next stage is to paint resin it prior to . . .

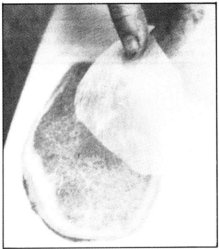

. . . applying a pre-cut piece of tissue.

paint boundary and when it is FULLY set ie. dry to the hand (don't forget there will still be a slight stickiness, but your hand will not stick to it), mix up your filler and spread it evenly over the tissue/resin and over the paint boundary. When it is set use 80/220 paper on a file or block to contour it; a second application of filler may be needed. Finally finish off with 220 grade paper because all spray fillers

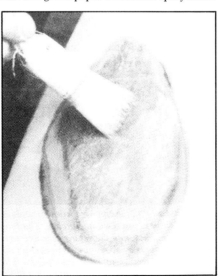

Tissue being "laminated" on.

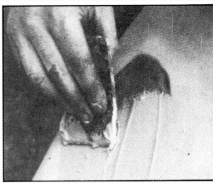

When all is thoroughly set, mix up the filler and make sure it is thoroughly mixed. Spread the filler over the repair evenly. Don't leave large tramlines all over it.

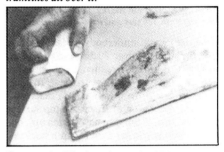

Contour the filler by using a "half file" by 3M or a cork block, both with P80 paper.

and hi-build primers are designed to take out the 220 marks.

The main potential faults are firstly, creating 'flats' on curved surfaces such as wings where when using a file it will work at a tangent to the curve instead of following it and, secondly, causing hollows in large flat panels ie. doors, bonnets, boot lids, where the panel will flex every time you rub and, consequently, you rub (dig) harder thus causing a hollow in the middle of the repair. Thirdly, not spending enough time ie. the resin is not fully set before applying the filler and, finally, the filler not mixed thoroughly; some areas gone off; some still soft and leaving grinding or score marks everywhere. All these defects will show up immediately when the repair is painted.

Remember, just one simple gel crack on, say, a bonnet will take from start to finish 45 minutes to one hour. Now, how many gel cracks have you found?

Compound damage

This type of damage, which requires laminating from behind, is fairly straightforward in that the top surface is always treated as a large gel crack. If there is a simple split, say, on a wheel arch, thoroughly clean the underside

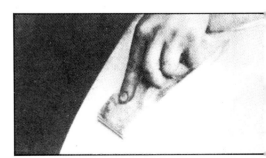

Flatting off with the 3M file.

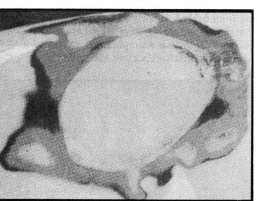

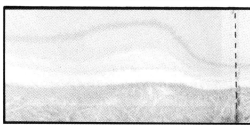

USING GLASS FIBRE

SURE it all correctly first BEFORE you cut it away. Use reference points ie. chassis fixings, bonnet, door openings, windscreen points, then cut off the damage and offer up the new piece. Local jiggling and cutting will result in the final fitting and, when you are satisfied, clamp (or rest) the new section in place temporarily and check the FIT of the door, bonnet etc.; do it BEFORE everything is stuck solid and you cannot shut the door. Prepare the old and new surface thoroughly, go back at least 12in beyond the join and then re-align and clamp on. Spread the load away

Removing all P80 marks and preparing for painting with 320 wet and dry — used wet.

of all debris and underbody sealant and use the grinderette with an 80 disc and abrade the surface to form a key, then go 3-4in either side of the split, and lay up these to form layers of 300 gr/m (old 1 oz/yd) mat, wait until it is fully set and attack the top surface as in part one. If the split has 'ridden up', one of two things can be done. Run a hacksaw blade or jig saw blade up the crack; this will remove the jagged edges and you can press the edges flush again. If the crack is severe then, after laminating underneath, grind into the new laminate on the top surface and use one layer of mat plus the tissue for the 'gel crack' repair.

For major compound fractures that don't require sections the area may have to be pieced together like a jig-saw using clamp plates to hold it fast. Always clamp from the top (painted surface) and laminate using four layers. When it is set, remove the plates and denib the screw surrounds with the grinderette. The structure is now sound again but the top is still a mess so grind the whole area and, if extensive, either drape one layer of matt plus tissue or two layers over this. When it is set fill as in the first part and get the contour right. Remember, the filler acts only as a veneer so it MUST NOT go on three inches deep because it will only crack away again. We have all seen superbly resprayed GRP cars which, given a slight 'ding' on a wheel arch, have shed two tons of filler from the entire wing due to a previous repair! All the strength of the repair is derived from

This picture illustrates a correctly feathered edge to the left of the line compared with the jagged edge (to the right) left by the grinder.

Using a jigsaw or hacksaw blade to "run the split" to make the two sides go down flat prior to preparing and laminating from behind.

laminating and filler is to give the cosmetic shape ONLY.

A fairly extensive compounded fracture on a rear wing/boot floor area will take about 10-20 hours to repair.

Major damage

Major accident damage which requires replacement sections can get complicated but buy only the repair section you actually need; don't buy a half front when all you require is a quarter front. Panic sets in at the thought of cutting off half of a car to bond on a new section but just remember to strip out everything around the bonding line and MEA-

from the join with at least four to five layers of laminate and, when it is set, remove the clamps, grind into the new laminate and then join and feather out to at least 8in-9in either side. Do it as described in part one but place two layers into the join and grade out, finally using tissue and filler. The join is inherently strong because you have made a whole new join with fresh laminate. NEVER just butt-join two sections as eventually a whole line will appear at the 'butt'. I've actually had an Elan rear section fall off where the owner had just butt-joined them up with one layer only underneath and filler on top. No one will ever know that a correctly fitted section has been put on. Approximate times for this type of repair (depending on the car) vary between 10-50 hours.

A final piece about 'bolt on' GRP panels, either to GRP cars or metal. With like-with-like bolt through panels on GRP cars use a silicone sealant between them first and use the largest washers available to spread the load. Do the same with metal or even sit the panel on a thin piece of isolating rubber strip; glazing rubber is ideal. If any panel has to be bonded on it is essential first to key the area well and use three to four layers graded out. On metal all rust must be removed and use a coarse disc 40 or 80 grade to provide the key; the bonding must be perfect with no air bubbles if possible, cross-bolt as well because metal always will expand and contract at different rates from GRP. Remember, NO STRUCTURAL METAL MUST EVER BE REPLACED BY GRP PANELS. Apart from the fact it is illegal, it is also highly dangerous.

All the foregoing has been condensed from my book 'How to restore Glassfibre Bodywork' published by Osprey and available at £7.50 from: Fibreglass Services, Charlton Saw Mills, Charlton, Chichester, West Sussex.   □

A mid front on a +2; the repair section extends to about halfway along the wheelarches. The bonnet was fitted first, and the repair area overlaps the original wings by about 6in. Always buy the correct repair section to meet your needs. The genuine factory sections have all the correct bobbins in them and they come ready primed.

All finished and ready for primer. Total time one hour. Note how large the repair area has now become compared with the original cracks.

NEXT MONTH:
Paint stripping and
preparing for the respray.

USING GLASS FIBRE

Painting GRP is not the same as painting metal and the quicker everybody realises this the better. The preparation required takes far longer as does the painting time so different painting techniques have to be applied. There are literally only a handful of professional GRP sprayers in the UK who achieve a finish that will last for at least 10 years or so.

Why does GRP painting differ so greatly from metal painting? The main reason is sinkage. GRP is a 'soft' material compared with metal and any repair NOT done properly will show due to the thinners in the painting process sinking into the GRP and then evaporating out, bringing the repair with it. Any excess of paint layers, ie. after about three resprays, will always show as a boundary around the repairs for this reason. The thinners will soften the receding layers of paint and lift the repair.

There are several matters arising from this. First, when doing a full repaint, if there is any shadow of doubt as to the soundness of the ORIGINAL factory paint, ie. microblistering or flaking off, or the car has had more than one or two resprays, it ALL HAS TO BE STRIPPED OFF. This cannot be stressed enough. Adopt any other approach to the problem and the end result will look terrible. You cannot paint over blisters, flaking paint etc. Secondly, all repairs must be done absolutely perfectly otherwise you're wasting your time and, thirdly, choose the paint scheme correctly, ie. stick with one system all the way through and use the same manufacturer, be it cellulose or the isocyanate 2K system (known as two-pack acrylics). Spraying cellulose systems requires a different technique from that used when spraying on metal; keep the thinner content to a minimum and build up the layers of paint almost dry. High thinner content will just flood the GRP surface to cause problems later on. If the original finish was cellulose use it again — nothing is worse than seeing an orange peel, lurid acrylic coloured Elan when it should be a flat-finished cellulose original factory colour.

Using the chisel to remove paint from the boot lid which is still attached to the car. When finished everything is removed from the car as explained in the text. ▶

The paint systems

It is worth mentioning the advantages and disadvantages of various paint schemes.

1. Cellulose — These have improved considerably over the past 15 years or so. Don't be bamboozled by the fast-talking sales rep about synthetic whizzos etc. They do NOT always understand about GRP but only about high volume spray shops dealing with Minis, Escorts etc. where turnround is all important. Cellulose was used (and still is of course) on all GRP cars up to the early '70s (Lotus changed to a polyurethane paint in '71 on their Elans etc.). So, first for originality on your classic, use it. Secondly it is easier to apply and can be blown-in locally if a mistake is made. Thirdly, a superb flat mirror finish can be achieved by

PART 4: Miles Wilkins concludes this series by looking at paint systems and preparation for painting.

Essential equipment: Paint remover, chisels, multi-sided scrapers, wet and dry papers, bucket, sponge and washing up liquid.

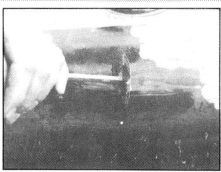

Scrape the paint off using a multi-sided scraper.

The paint is so thick here that chiselling was the best way. Keep the blade as flat as possible to minimise the risk of digging through to the gel coat.

Flatting the area by hand down to the bare GRP.

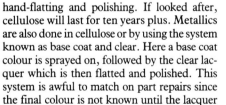

Painting on the stripper. Note the reaction bubbles; some paints will not do this — the stripper just softening the surface — leave on for 5-10 minutes.

Coming now to the first primer coat (white) and an old repair.

Flatting off by hand with 220 grade paper back to bare GRP on this three-quarter panel. Sponge is squeezed to supply a constant dribble of water. Eventually the whole car has to look like this.

hand-flatting and polishing. If looked after, cellulose will last for ten years plus. Metallics are also done in cellulose or by using the system known as base coat and clear. Here a base coat colour is sprayed on, followed by the clear lacquer which is then flatted and polished. This system is awful to match on part repairs since the final colour is not known until the lacquer has been painted on.

2. Two-pack acrylic-isocyanates. Quite simply do NOT spray these yourself as external breathing apparatus is required. The fumes given off are lethal. Either use new isocyanate-free paint (only available in a few colours as yet) or get a professional firm to spray it for you. The advantages of this system are that it minimises sinkage (no thinner content) and it is more durable in service. Its disadvantages include the fact that it cannot be part blown in on a repair so the whole panel has to be done. It is very difficult to lose

an edge and, unless flatted and polished within 24 hours, an orange peel finish will remain.

3. Synthetics. Nobody in their right mind uses these air- or chemical-drying plastic paints on a classic car. They provide a very cheap way of obtaining a shine and may be ideal for kit cars etc. but are virtually impossible to repair over and, as with acrylics, the edge cannot be lost. The whole panel has to be painted.

Do not bake

It is time that everyone, professionals included, realised that YOU CANNOT LOW BAKE ANY GRP CAR. Numerous

bodies have been lost in this way and people still do it. A true low bake is 130°C. At that temperature, even for half an hour, the body will flow and become useless. The maximum temperature for any scheme is a FORCE DRY 85-110°F which is 30-40°C. I have had to arbitrate on several occasions on behalf of owners whose cars have suffered GRP flow after being painted by professionals.

What it costs

I repeat, GRP painting is very different from painting metal and it costs two or three times as much. There is no such thing as a 'cheap

(Continued)

(Continued)

£400 blowover'. The true cost among my professional 'friends', including ourselves, starts around £1500 to £2500 for a strip and repaint on, say, a Europa. Realistically the finished cost is over £3000 which includes new rubbers, rehanging doors etc. IT IS NOT CHEAP TO DO IT PROPERLY and to do it properly is the only way.

Preparing/removing the old paint

Now for the awful bit! Having decided the course of action for the repaint you have a choice of methods of preparation depending on circumstances:

1. The lazy one first — on self-coloured gel coat cars, namely kit cars or bolt-on GRP wings/panels etc., if any repairs have to be done, do as outlined last month. Then flat off the whole car/panel with 360 wet and dry (wet with a little washing up liquid in it) to provide the key. Dry thoroughly and then it is ready for the painting process.

2. If the original paint is sound or you elect not to strip it all off, repair the cracks/damage/marks etc. first, then REMOVE EVERYTHING from the car that can be removed ie. door frames, glass, lights, the lot, and flat off the entire car with 360, paying particular attention to the repair/paint boundaries. These areas must be absolutely perfect. Use lots of water and change the paper regularly. If the carpets/seats are still left in, cover them up well because wet coloured stains are quite difficult to remove when the crud has dried! Finally, when all has been flatted, wash with clean warm water and dry thoroughly.

3. Stripping a whole car will take a very, very long time whichever method you choose. People just do not realise the hundreds of hours it takes. Unlike metal where you can apply paint stripper everywhere and high pressure hose it off, paint stripper attacks GRP so extra care has to be taken. If using the paint stripper method buy the water soluble stripper only. Do NOT buy the special GRP ones that are intended for marine purposes only. They do not remove cellulose/acrylics. If you are stripping an original finish take it off BY HAND. DO NOT use paint stripper because, if you do, one pass of the scraper and you'll be through. Start with 80 grade wet and dry finishing with 220 and 360.

Before starting with paint stripper first de-wax the car with petrol or solvent but be sure to eliminate all risk of fire. Wipe clean and then key the surface with 80 grade paper to provide a grip for the stripper otherwise the first applications will remove only the remaining wax polish! Work on a small area at a time and scrape the paint down to the original primer coat only. Always leave doors, boot lid etc. attached to the car because it is easier to work on these when they are anchored in position.

When you have finished with the stripper take off the door handles, frames, glass, lights etc. and finish around these points by hand with wet and dry paper. Taking everything off first may seem logical but you do not

USING GLASS FIBRE

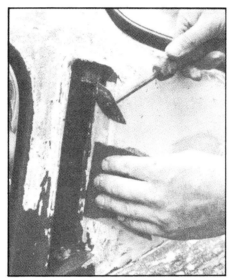

Using paper or a multi-sided scraper for the awkward bits.

want stripper all inside the car eating into vinyl seats etc. and the build-up of unremoved stripper in and around door handle holes etc. will give horrible paint problems later on. After each patch has been done thoroughly, wash off with water to neutralise the stripper. Go over the whole car, leaving any old repairs — do not paint strip them out. When the car is, hopefully, in its original primer, flat off by hand with wet 220 wet and dry. Next wash the entire car and then TACKLE THE REPAIRS both old and new (gel cracks show up as dark yellow lines). Finally flat off again totally with wet 360 grade wet and dry and the car should be ready for painting.

Chipping off the paint using chisels is an alternative to paint stripper. This can sometimes prove to be quicker provided that the paint comes off easily. You will find this method is best when the car has many layers of paint. Use a 1in wide chisel (maximum) or smaller sizes for the fiddly bits. Do not gouge into the GRP. If you do scrape too far and remove the gel coat treat the area as a gel crack for repair. This applies also to gouges made when using paint stripper.

Another method of stripping is by hand-sanding. This will really take forever, especially if you have to take off six repaints; to use an electric orbital sander or equivalent is a waste of time. NEVER be tempted to use a grinderette or a cintride disc as these will tear through the paint and straight into the GRP. By far the quickest method is to use a compressed air orbital sander starting with 40

Definitely a case for stripping. This Europa has suffered the ravages of time and loads of repaints.

grade paper and working down to 220 grade. The flexible backing pad will allow awkward corners and curves to be reached. Be careful when nearing the initial primer coat. Stop and take this off by hand otherwise, after painting, you'll wonder why the beautiful gloss finish has a myriad of squiggles all over it.

Further Reading

"How to Restore Fibreglass Bodywork" and "How to Restore Paintwork", both by Miles Wilkins and published in the Osprey Restoration Guide series. Both of these books can be obtained direct from Miles at £7.95 each including postage and packing and his address is Fibreglass Services, Charlton Saw Mills, Charlton, Singleton, near Chichester, West Sussex.

For the bare body use ICI (or Glasurit) spray filler. This is designed to take out 80 grade marks and is self-etching. I never use Lessanol as I believe that it can cause problems later on. DO NOT use spray fillers over painted surfaces but only over the repairs. After the spray filler use high build primers and then your colour. Or, if the body is perfect, use a two-pack primer (which should prevent sinkage) and then your colour whether cellulose or two-pack scheme.

On a final note, it usually takes about 250 hours to strip and paintspray a Lotus Elan +2. If you have done it yourself you have probably found that it has taken hours more. Painting and polishing alone in a cellulose scheme will account for around 70-80 hours of that time.

□

The final result. All the body was stripped and repaired and 16 coats of colour applied, flatted off after every four and finally hand-polished.

Flashing the Scimitar

Chris Graham introduces his new staff car

Pictures by Chris Graham

Back in the days when I was an impressionable nipper who used to wear mauve shirts with wide collars, collect Slade, Sweet and Suzi Quatro singles and make horrible noises on a Rolf Harris Stylophone, my appreciation of cars was somewhat limited. However, one motoring memory from that time, which has remained with me to this day, is that of a car owned by a friend's father. It was big, shiny and green with a rumbly engine and comfy seats. It could go fast without revving loudly and seemed to speed round all corners with ease. It was a Reliant Scimitar GTE.

A few months ago when the time came for a change of staff car I was undecided about what to get. The trusty Volvo 244 had served me with loyal devotion but, unfortunately, its classic status was zero which severely limited its relevance as a *Practical Classics* staff car. For ages I had toyed with various ideas – a Mk2 Lotus Cortina, a Triumph 2.5PI, a P6 Rover 3.5S – and then I remembered, with affection, that green Scimitar from years ago. It had everything I wanted. Stylish looks, a 'lazy' V6-engine, a reasonable degree of comfort for long journeys, a rot-free body and reliable running gear. Yes, I had decided – I wanted one!

The problem, as ever, was to find a good example. So many of the Scimitars on the road these days are in an appalling state with chipped and crazed bodywork and uncared-for trim. This, I am convinced, stems from the fact that complacent owners feel no compunction to remedy body damage simply because they are dealing with glass fibre and not rust-prone metal.

Choosing the model was difficult. I was torn between the SE5, which was introduced in 1969 and is generally regarded as the 'best of the bunch', and the SE6. The latter, which appeared in 1975, features a longer, wider bodyshell with improved interior trim and better sound deadening. There are arguments for and against both models. The SE5s have awful lights, cheap trim but great performance and road holding. For their part the SE6s are more refined but body-flexing can be a problem (because of the enlargments) and many consider the engine cooling system inadequate. However, as it turned out, a good SE6 presented itself first and so the decision was taken for me.

On a cold and drizzly November morning Paul Skilleter and I set off in the editorial Bentley to the Attleborough Scimitar Centre in Norfolk (The Garage, Norwich Road, Besthorpe, Attleborough, Norfolk NR17 2LB, Tel: 0953 455556). Despite the efforts of the terribly congested A11 the Bentley, which had just enjoyed an involved cylinder head gasket change, performed admirably and we arrived in a suitably dignified and un-flustered frame of mind.

The car we had come to see, a 1976 manual (with o/d) SE6, was on the forecourt and certainly looked smart. The body, finished in brown with an oatmeal-coloured vinyl roof, was in excellent condition compared with most you see on the roads. The chrome was also good and all other trim and badging was present. I was pleased to see that it was run-

The Scimitar is very comfortable to drive although taller occupants will suffer from the lack of headroom. Instrumentation is good and provides details on speed, revs, oil pressure, fuel, water temperature, amps and time. The four switches beneath the clock and radio operate heated rear window, hazard lights, main lights and rear fog lights. The two below the ventilators control the intensity of gauge illumination and the rear wash/wipe. The car is fitted with electric windows and they are operated by switches just behind the gear lever on the central arm rest/oddment compartment.

The spare wheel occupies pride of place under the bonnet. It's almost as though the engine was shoe-horned in as an afterthought!

The happy day! Barry Herber presents me with the keys on a bitterly cold day in Norfolk.

ning on the attractive optional alloy wheels (a la the MGB V8) rather than the standard steel ones with those nasty cheap glass fibre trims. Inside, the light tan nylon cloth seat facings and matching cockpit trimming were generally in good order and a few cigarette burns and one tear on the seats were the only real signs of age. After a quick initial inspection and chat with Barry Herber, the proprieter there, we hitched on the trade plates and set off up the road to see what the car could do.

Immediately we were impressed by its feel. It was tight and largely rattle-free although there was a noticeable clonk from the rear as the power was taken up after each gear change. Much to my relief the optional power steering was not present. Reliant apparently had troubles with the system used on the early SE6s and many owners complained that it was far too light. The gearbox felt a bit notchy by modern standards and the long travel between gears, which is not exactly conducive to speedy changes, took some getting used to. On the other hand the overd-

rive, which operates on third and fourth, was one of the smoothest that I have experienced and both Paul and I agreed that the car was a real pleasure to drive.

When we returned to the garage Barry gave us a glowing report on what had been done to the car (new brake shoes and pads, front suspension overhaul, new stainless steel exhaust, full service etc.) and this, coupled with how we felt about it, secured the deal. The price we paid was £2,995 and, although we realise that this is quite expensive for an SE6 of this age, we feel that its overall condition and degree of originality make the price quite justifiable.

Homeward bound

Setting off for home was exciting. The car was completely new to me and, apart from a couple of brief drives in a friend's SE5, my experience with Scimitars was very limited. Everything went well until, in between the crackles and hisses of the aged radio, I managed by chance to catch a travel flash warning of a serious accident at the Dartford Tunnel. Such news strikes fear into the hearts of even the most seasoned M25 users let alone people like me driving unfamiliar, large-engined classic cars. The announcer suggested avoiding the tunnel for the next hour so, without argument, I beat a hasty retreat to the nearest Little Chef. Suitably refreshed I sped off down the M11 and swept on to the M25 bound for the dreaded tunnel.

Everything was fine until I got within three miles of the 'hole' and saw a wall of red lights ahead. My heart sank as I joined the jam and I fixed my nervous gaze on the all-important temperature gauge. To my horror it was up to 90 degrees in a flash and rising steadily. I switched the heater – and I use the term lightly – to full speed but still the needle marched on. Knowing what was about to happen I made my way to the inside lane and

The Scimitar has a useful luggage carrying capacity – the rear seats fold forward to give the maximum room. Owners who are more than 5ft 5in tall may encounter problems when stooping in underneath the rear window. I have hit my head a number of times already!

In my opinion the Scimitar is a well proportioned car. However, the design of the sloping rear window means that it is continually dirty in bad weather – the wipe/wash is a very necessary fitment.

prepared to abandon ship. At the first sign of steam I pulled on to the hard shoulder and switched off. I sat dejected and consciously avoiding the smug glances from the modern motorists who I could sense were grinning at me and my crippled classic.

It was quite apparent that the electrically operated cooling fan was not working. Of course, I had no tools with me and, since the fan is located beneath a bolted metal tray which supports the spare wheel under the bonnet, there was little to be done but wait until it cooled. A kindly fellow Scimitar owner stopped to give encouragement but it was obvious that I wasn't going anywhere until the traffic had eased sufficiently to give me a clear run at the tunnel. Eventually, after messing about for one-and-a-half hours I got through and scuttled off home, paying more than special attention to all the dials as I went.

Teething troubles

Since then a few other problems have arisen. The clutch pedal loses pressure every now and then even though the level in the master cylinder is as it should be. In addition, there is a tapping noise which seems to relate to the clutch because it slows down and disappears when the pedal is depressed. In the mornings reverse gear is sometimes a struggle to select.

While rushing to smarten up the car for some colour photography I made the mistake of running it through a car wash. This highlighted most effectively that the door rubbers are past it. Water and foam cascaded in around the tops of the doors and my pitiful efforts with a small handkerchief did little to save the seats and my trousers from a soaking! Fortunately it has not rained since I have had the car but, seeing as the car cannot be garaged, it is important that the rubbers are replaced before the weather gets really wet.

The handbrake is rather ineffective but I am sure that this is just a matter of adjustment. The same applies to the headlamps. The seven inch lamps used when on dipped beam are quite good but their current positioning produces a couple of 'hot spots' about 20 feet in front and very little else. They may well benefit from some halogen bulbs and readjustment.

I have investigated the problem with the fan. Originally I thought that the trouble lay with the heat-controlled switch plugged into the side of the radiator. However, this was not case. It does work because the fan can be coaxed into life when the engine reaches about 90 degrees C. The problem is that the motor is clogged-up with road dirt thrown up through the wire mesh beneath it and it needs to be completely stripped and cleaned. In the meantime I have 'attacked' it with good old WD40 which will hopefully allow it to run more freely until it can be seen to properly. Up until now I have been stopping the car every time it gets hot, rushing round to the front armed with a thin stick and prodding the fan into life up through the wire mesh under the air dam! It reminds me of that scene from the ever-funny Fawlty Towers series when Basil, in utter desperation, threatens and then thrashes his poor old Austin 1100 with the branch of a tree. I just hope that over the next few months I am not driven to a similar performance! □

Staff Car Sagas

Chris Graham gets the niggles

Well, the niggles are back! After some two years of virtually trouble-free Volvo motoring I am pleased to report that it's business as usual again on the staff car front. The **Reliant Scimitar** has been misbehaving already but, before I tell you how, I must start by saying that, overall, I am delighted with the car; it feels great to have a classic staff car again!

The problem with the electric cooling fan described last month was not cured by my endeavours with a screwdriver and can of WD40. I was unable to remove the fan blades from the motor because my poor-quality Allen key distorted and then spun merrily within the festered grub screw securing it. This unsatisfactory situation brought to a halt any hopes I had had of stripping the motor to clean it because, with the blades in place, it is impossible to get the thing apart. In search of relief I took the car to Scimitar specialist Nigel Newth-Gibbs (1A Park Lane, Aveley, Essex RM15 4UD, Tel: 0708 867900/866563). I was pleased to note that Nigel, who runs the business with his brother and a part-time helper, was reasonably impressed with the car. He wasted little time in swapping the old encrusted fan motor for a new one and took care to ensure that he fitted the blades correctly. Obviously they must blow air on to the radiator rather than suck it away – apparently a frequent mistake made by owners.

Another niggle concerned the passenger's door release mechanism. Right from the start

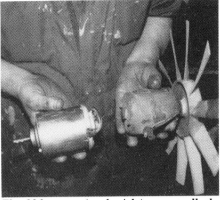

The old fan motor (on the right) was actually the wrong type. Mounting brackets had been sawn crudely from the barrel to make it fit. The replacement has worked faultlessly ever since.

this was tricky to operate and it gradually worsened until opening it from the inside was impossible. Having to rush round and open the door for my female passengers did wonders for my gentlemanly image but doing the same for characters like Peter Simpson was considerably less agreeable! Nigel removed the door trim panel but could not see anything obviously wrong. Then he realised the cause of the problem – the door had dropped.

I had a feeling that Nigel did not relish the prospect of loosening the hinges and re-hanging the door and, after two hours of intense struggling, I realised why. The SE6 is famous for its 'door drop' (extra strengthening was added to the A post on the SE6a) but in this case the story is a little more complicated. After loosening, adjusting and re-tightening the hinges for about the fiftieth time Nigel came to the conclusion that the door aperture was the wrong shape. Then, after carefully examining the ripply front nearside wing he found evidence to suggest that the whole lot

The original thermostat was a bit 'sticky' and so was replaced.

had been replaced at some stage and that it hadn't been done terribly well.

A join at the front was visible (eight inches to the right of the badge) and, at the rear nearside corner of the bonnet aperture, the other joint was starting to crack back across the scuttle top towards the windscreen. The worst of it was that the A post had not been aligned correctly during the repair which now makes it impossible to hang the door accurately. Wind noise and draughts seem now to be inevitable. Anyway, at least the door now opens from the inside.

Over the Christmas break the car let me down three times. Admittedly, two of these were due to nothing more than a flat battery. I tracked this down to a loose fan belt which was failing to drive the alternator. Fortunately, there was plently of adjustment left on the bracket and loosening the bolt and swinging the alternator further out seems to have done the trick. The third breakdown was rather more serious. While visiting friends in Poole, Dorset, I suddenly 'lost' third and fourth gears. First, second and reverse were fine but where third and fourth should have been there was nothing. Typically, this happened on an occasion when I had no tools with me and even my overalls had mysteriously disappeared.

I presumed that the problem lay with the selector mechanism but didn't fancy grovelling around under the car to find out. Fortunately, I knew a man who did....I telephoned the AA! Allen Buckingham, who patrols the Bournemouth area as well as occasionally reading *PC*, arrived in next to no time and we immediately set about removing the transmission tunnel trim to see what lay below the gear lever. This turned out to be a waste of

The Scimitar was squeezed into Nigel Newth-Gibbs' 'compact' workshop in Essex for some of his special attention.

time because we discovered that the problem lay under the car. Immediately beneath the gear lever there is the gearchange control assembly which transmits the movements of the lever down the correct selector rod under the car to the selector lever on the gearbox. The joint between the selector rod and lever is secured with a small pin and spring clip which, in my case, had sprung off. Miraculously though, the tiny clip was still clinging gamely to the selector rod and so Allan had the two back together in a jiffy! Three cheers for the AA!

On a more sober note I must end with an item of concern. The Scimitar's engine has rather a worrying appetite for water. I am topping it up every week so, quite obviously, there is a leak somewhere. While the car was at Nigel's workshop we noticed that there were signs of coolant loss from the water pump so replacing this, and probably the gaskets too, is a job for the future.   □

Chris Graham reflects on a bad start

I think that it is fair to say that I have not been blessed with the best of luck so far in my exploits with the **Reliant Scimitar**. Not long after acquiring the car I was hit by a grumpy young woman in a Mini. She pulled out of her drive, through a line of stationary traffic, and proceeded to try to turn right as I was passing in the outside lane. Her car lurched out into my nearside door with a sickening crunch. Fortunately there was nothing coming the other way and I was able to swerve out and away from her which minimised the damage. However, I am pleased to say that the glassfibre of the Scimitar took the impact well and did not crack although the door is noticeably battle-scarred. The Grumpymobile was rather more crumpled.

Events then reached a new low a few weeks later when some little so-and-so broke into the car and stole my £110 tripod. Leaving work one evening I reached the car only to discover that the offside rear quarter window was smashed and that a hole had been punched in the middle through which my tripod had been extracted. The granules of laminated glass were thrown all over the interior. The little b*****d bent the chrome window surround, presumably in an ignorant effort to try to prise it open, before losing patience and simply smashing it in. The road where the car was parked is in a particularly

At first I was proud of my temporary window. It was water-tight and stayed in place at all speeds.

lush part of Beckenham and on the route taken by children going to and from a nearby school – I am sure that one of them was

responsible. Incidents like this only confirm my views that, thanks to the new generation of ill-disciplined 'people' motivated by ignorance, greed and mindless envy, the outlook for the law-abiding citizen in this country becomes ever more bleak.

After a drafty and irritating drive home I set about masking up the window with a sheet of polythene and black insulating tape.

However, my opinion changed when I came to remove the insulating tape and the paint came away with it. Thank goodness I hadn't put more on the bodywork.

Nigel Newth-Gibbs (Tel: 0708 867900) turned up trumps by locating a secondhand glass for me. It cost only £10 and, a few days later, I snatched a spare hour and went over to his Essex workshop to pick it up. Just as things were starting to look up another disaster struck. As I removed the insulating tape from the body I was shocked to reveal gleaming white glassfibre – yes, I had pulled the paint off with the tape. I felt like crying! Even lifting it as carefully and slowly as possible made no difference and the paint came away like the skin off a rice pudding.

I realise, of course, that the problem of smash and grab with the Scimitar is always going to be with me because there is no conventional boot. However, I understand that a rear tonneau to cover the loading bay was an optional extra originally. One of these would certainly help. One preventive measure I have taken already is that I have started to use a clever little 'fake alarm' device. The unit, which is available by mail order from Tiron Marketing (PO Box 75, Stevenage, Herts. SG1 5QB), plugs into the cigarette lighter socket and a flashing LED mounted on top does a very creditable impression of an alarm indicator. Obviously the device is only effective at night when, short of shining a torch in, all that can be seen is the blinking red light.

There is still a nagging electrical fault which manifests itself if the car is left, unused, for more than 24 hours – all the charge in the battery drains away. The battery, which I have tested, appears to be in good condition so I can only assume that there is a slow leak somewhere else in the circuitry. There is certainly a wiring mix-up at the rear because I only have one brake light working when the side/headlights are switched on.   □

Chris Graham struggles on

Things are going pretty well for me at the moment, generally speaking. My promotion to the Editorial chair (or bench seeing as I share it with Peter Simpson!) has lifted my spirits and freshened my outlook. Derby County finished well up in the First Division,

the summer weather appears to be with us and, best of all, I managed completely to miss the dreaded Eurovision Song Contest! In fact the only cloud on the horizon at the moment is the jolly old **Reliant Scimitar**. It continues to be a regular source of trouble.

Kim Henson (my knight in shining armour!) stands proudly beside the stricken Scimitar brandishing his Polish pliers. His trolley jack had an interesting history too and needed a pair of Botswanan Mole grips to release it!

The worst incident in recent months was a repitition of the gear linkage failure. It happened in Poole (again!) on the way back from a photographic session. I went to change from third to top but, as before, the gearlever flapped around with disconcerting ease – the gears were nowhere to be found. I knew exactly what had happened and, although the car was stuck in third gear, I managed to get up a hill, round a roundabout and on to the forecourt of a petrol station. As luck would have it the garage was one of the new generation with multi-grade computer controlled pumps, air hoses, car vacuums, piped music, a supermarket but, of course, not a workshop with friendly mechanic in sight!

The car had to be lifted to get at the linkage but the only means I had of doing this was to use the car's weedy scissor jack which I did not trust. So I made an SOS telephone call to Kim Henson who lives locally and who I knew would have a trolley jack. Within minutes he arrived with said jack, axle stands, spare overalls and a selection of tools.

Underneath, it was apparent that exactly the same had happened as before (Staff Car Sagas, March '89) and, once again, the offending spring clip was still miraculously stuck to the selector rod. Kim was amazed at the amount of wear and play in the linkages as I set about re-connecting the two ends. We decided, in true *Practical Classics* style, to secure the clip temporarily with a piece of string which we found in the boot of Kim's car. Although a bit Heath Robinson, the repair lasted well until the joint was wired up more securely at a later date.

I have also had more problems with the cooling system. As you already know, the engine is drinking water by the pint – the major causes are, I think, a tired water pump and seeping radiator. I have tried several radiator sealant additives but all to no avail. However, the water really hit the fan so to speak when, after a long, hot journey through south London, the top heater hose burst. The water was leaking out too quickly to drive any distance so I had to stop at a garage which luckily had a replacement length of hose.

The old length of hose was held on with

two of the oldest and most decrepit Jubilee clips you could ever wish to see. The most awkward one to remove secured the hose to a short length metal pipe which stuck out about three quarters of an inch through a hole low down in the centre of the bulkhead. It was very hard to get any purchase on the screwdriver while working at arms length but eventually, several skinned knuckles later, I managed to free it. Little did I know it but this was the easy part. Replacing the new hose with the old clip was even harder. After about an hour of spasmodic struggling I thought I had done it, replaced the air filter and its casing, packed up my tools and set off for home. I got there but, as soon as I switched off the engine, I could here an ominous hissing – water was leaking around the bulkhead joint. I had to let it cool and start all over again. This time I swapped Jubilee clips and my efforts were rewarded with a leak-free seal.

Other problems with the car have included seized seat belt mechanisms, sticking tailgate lock, jammed seat tilting mechanism, faulty driver's window motor and a gradually worsening rear axle. It's quite fun sitting here and wondering whether there is anything else left on the car to go wrong!

Chris Graham looses his cool, again!

After enjoying a few hundred miles of virtually trouble-free motoring the **Scimitar** made a repeat performance of one of its favourite and, I must say, most effective tricks the other day. It unceremoniously dumped the contents of its cooling system all over the office car park for the second time in a matter of weeks. On this occasion the cause was traced to a perished rubber blanking plug

The Scimitar sits contentedly at Stanford Hall while, no doubt, plotting its next jolly jape!

located on top of the water pump. This is held in place with a Jubilee clip and blocks off a water outlet which, presumably, finds a use when the pump is fitted to cars which have a proper heater! Fortunately, the offending item turned out to be a Ford part which was replaced for the bargain price of just 18p and I was back in business.

The car's thirst for water has increased dramatically recently and, at present, I am having to pour in about two pints every day!. I know that the radiator is seeping but doubt if this is to blame now. Regrettably, we have started to think about blown gaskets and distorted heads as possible causes. Oh dear! As if this isn't enough there is a further disconcerting occurrence which I noticed recently. The water temperature shoots up well above normal as the engine warms from cold before it settles back down to a comfortable level. I

suspect that the thermostat might have become 'overcooked' thus preventing it from opening when it should. Still, if this is the case it is the least of my worries and is a simple matter to put right. Sooner or later I fear that we are going to have to carry out a major investigation into the true state of this engine. Carrying out minor repair after minor repair seems just to be pouring good money after bad.

On a happier note I am grateful to Barry Herber, from the Attleborough Scimitar Centre, Norfolk, (Tel: 0953 455556) who, after reading about the theft from my car, kindly supplied me with one of the original tonneau covers for the load space behind the rear seats. I can now rest more easily at night knowing that my personal bits are covered up!

So far, since I acquired the car last November, I have covered some 11,500 miles and, although there have been numerous problems, this motoring has been enjoyable. There is a great cammeradarie between Scimitar owners on the road and you can always expect to see enthusiastic waving and headlamp flashing when cars meet. In addition, I have had a heartening response from readers offering helpful advice and suggestions. I can assure you that all are noted and acted upon when possible.

Chris Graham gets thirsty

As I sit before the word processor to bash out this latest episode in the long-running Scimitar saga, my throat is parched and the temperature in the office is almost unbearable. We are in the grips of a water shortage and much of south London is relying on strategically placed 500-gallon tanks for its supply. Hose pipes are banned and there are helicopter patrols out looking for suspiciously green back gardens. Private car washing is, of course, frowned upon although I am continually astonished to find the giant car wash machines at most garages still up and running and using water like there's no tomorrow. It's hard for the general public to take the shortage seriously when they see the likes of bowling clubs watering their precious greens for 12 hours at a time – surely the priorities are wrong somewhere along the line.

Anyway, it is with considerable guilt that I have to continue pouring pint after pint of

precious water down the **Reliant Scimitar's** greedy gullet. It's appetite is insatiable. The radiator was re-cored a couple of weeks ago after the old one finally sprang a terminal leak. The chaps down at South London Radiators Ltd (r/o 10-14 Bromley Road, Beckenham, Kent, Tel: 01-650 8986) made the switch in return for £92 and I fondly imagined that my troubles were over. They checked the rest of the cooling system, too, but found nothing else wrong. The thermostat and all hoses were fine. However, doubts were expressed about the condition of the head gaskets and this confirmed one of my worst fears. On past occasions I have seen water and steam hissing out from around the gasket at one point – not a particularly inspiring sight!

Now that the radiator is working properly it has increased the pressure on the rest of the system and, I'm afraid, worsened the problem with the gaskets. The engine is still using an unacceptable amount of water and it seems unlikely that it is leaking from anywhere else. Somewhat surprisingly though, there is no sign, on the dipstick anyway, of water in the oil. Perhaps, thinking about it, this is because the car has such a quick throughput of oil that there is no time for any noticeable amount of water to build up before the oil is consumed!

As soon as I have to time to get it organised, the car will be sent to Queensbury Road Garage, Kettering (Tel: 0536 513351) where their experts will give the engine the once-over. If things look too grim I shall probably opt for a replacement unit.

Yet another failure occurred on the way down to Dorset a few weeks ago when the overdrive packed up. Now it does not work at all in third gear and only occasionally, for short spells, in top. When it does work it is perfectly normal for a few seconds and then it disengages itself. I've given up trying to use it at all for the time being. Without the overdrive the engine uses about 500rpm more which is very noticeable at motorway speeds. It's much noisier and uses more fuel.

Apart from a faulty light switch which results in the instruments not being illuminated at night the rest of the car is fine. I still get great pleasure from driving it and it is certainly a car in which you can put up very respectable journey times in reasonable comfort. On the open road the heavy steering and clutch and the clumsy gearchange are less noticeable. It is definitely most at home when touring. □

KEEPING YOUR COOL

Alan Moore describes his own solutions to the notorious Reliant Scimitar overheating problems

To many Scimitar owners, keeping ears pricked for that ominous hiss, gurgle, gurgle, hiss of a boiling engine is all part and parcel of Reliant motoring. Thinking you've sorted out the problem only for the blessed thing to boil up again is irritating in the extreme and it always seems to happen when you've forgotten your can of water! Still, take heart, read on and learn how I have cured the water loss and boiling problems on my SE6 once and for all.

Water loss and overheating are always aggravated by a lack of maintenance but often questionable design has an effect too. In the case of the Reliant Scimitar SE6 one of the problems is that the radiator is positioned lower than the cylinder head. This means that there is no air space at the top of the radiator to allow for water expansion and this causes problems. The following details are specific to the Scimitar but the principles apply to any water-cooled car; Imp and V8 P6 owners please note!

Starting from basics the first part of the solution involves discovering the degree to which water expands when it is heated and then finding suitable space to allow for this and the displaced air. Solving these problems means that, in principle, the pressure cap should never have to let anything in or out.

My reference book shows that between 5 deg C and 100 deg C water expands by a factor of 0.04332. This means that, in the case of the Scimitar, the 17 pints of coolant will increase in volume by 0.47 pints. Measuring the capacity of the original catch tank provided by Reliant reveals its volume to be 1½ pints. Yet for some reason, often as not, it does not work. This is obviously not due to a lack of capacity so what is the cause?

Identification

The proper pressure cap has two seals on it. The bottom one pressurises the radiator and the other provides the seal to ensure the contents of the catch tank are sucked back into the radiator when it all cools down. This sits directly under the top of the cap. The slightest leak on the top seal means that the contents are not returned to the radiator upon cooling. The next time the engine is run, because there is no header tank, a mixture of air and water will be circulated. This is a recipe for further water loss which will eventually cause overheating. Of course, good maintenance will go a long way to solving the problem but it is better to keep all the water inside the cooling system.

Pressurised expansion space is required to solve the problem. This can be achieved by

It took Alan about three months to sort out the cooling on his Reliant Scimitar.

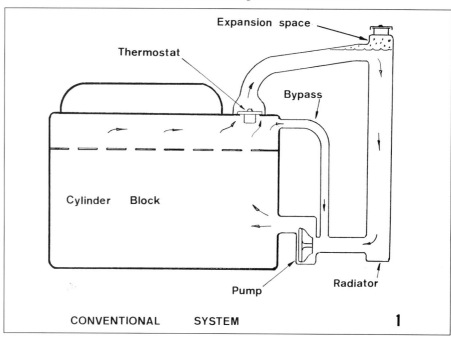

fitting a header tank directly to the cylinder head or connecting a separate tank from the bottom hose with a small air bleed pipe between the tank and the thermostat housing. Technically the best solution is to connect the expansion tank to the bottom hose. This is because air bled to it will stay in the tank. With the expansion tank on top of the cylinder head, it is possible for air to be picked up and circulated by the water.

It is also better to fill the system from the bottom because less air will be trapped this way. The bottom connected tank can also be of larger capacity, so giving greater latitude for slightly leaky systems. For the same reason it is advisable to keep the catch tank associated with the cylinder head-mounted expansion tank. Note, the top of the separate expansion tank must be higher than the outlet for the bleed pipe on the thermostat housing.

I have an expansion tank fitted to the cylinder head (manufactured by Robin Rew at Silverstone) on my engine. For those who wish to make their own system, or those who want to solve a cooling problem on any other car, I have done some detailed calculations. My sums are for the Reliant Scimitar but they are applicable to any other leak-proof system. Calculating the expansion space first: One pint of water occupies 34.6cu in. The 'Rew pot' is 4in in diameter giving 12.57cu in of water per inch of height. So the expansion height required works out at almost exactly 2in.

In theory any Ford V6 system will not lose water if there is about 3/4 pint of space available for water expansion. However, on each temperature cycle, air will be expelled via the pressure cap and most likely coolant with it so, to guarantee no coolant loss, space for the air to be compressed needs to

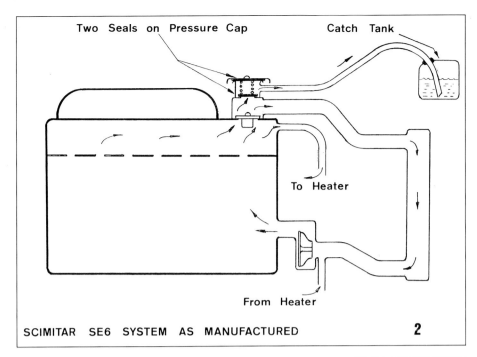

Two Seals on Pressure Cap

Catch Tank

To Heater

From Heater

SCIMITAR SE6 SYSTEM AS MANUFACTURED   **2**

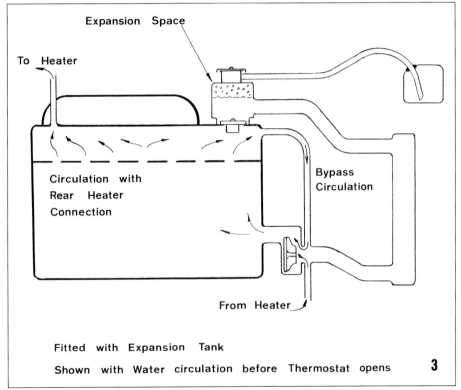

Expansion Space

To Heater

Circulation with
Rear Heater
Connection

**Bypass
Circulation**

From Heater

Fitted with Expansion Tank

Shown with Water circulation before Thermostat opens   **3**

When buying a Scimitar it's a good idea to check the area around the catch tank. This is mounted in front of the brake master cylinder. Suspect a blown head gasket if the surrounding bodywork is stained with rusty water.

This picture looks down on top of the radiator, the spare wheel having been removed. A convenient point to mount the fan control switch is on a bracket bolted to the radiator mounting plate. Fitting the sensor bulb in the radiator end of the top hose as shown isolates the pipe from vibration.

be found as well. Referring again to my reference book it gives a formula for the compression of air which says that the compressed volume of air is equal to the initial absolute pressure multiplied by 0.71, multiplied by the initial volume. The answer is that 8.87cu in of compression space is needed. Converting this volume to height for the 'Rew' pot gives 0.7in. Multiplying the cubic inches per pint by the SE6's expansion volume and, adding the air space volume, actually comes out to one pint. So, a free air space height of 2.7in will allow for all expansion of water and compression of air. No air or water should ever leave the system and it should be possible to leave off the catch tank.

It must be made clear that, while nothing should come out of the system, it must NOT be considered sealed. A sealed system would explode if, for instance, the head gasket leaked. Also the pressure cap rating specified by the vehicle manufacturer must be used. This is 13psi for the Scimitar SE6.

Having apparently made the system leak-proof it may still use water. Why? On the Ford V6 water might get into the motor past the gasket between the inlet manifold and head. There is a significant difference between the coefficients of expansion of cast iron and aluminium. A quite crude sum suggests that between a hot and cold engine the differential expansion across the top of the 'V' inlet manifold amounts to about 0.01in. This is about the thickness of four pages of this magazine.

This change in size between the cast iron and aluminium is restrained by the clamping force of the securing bolts. The resulting very high levels of stress are transferred through the gasket; thus a certain amount of movement may take place each time the engine heats and cools. My guess is that when the engine cools the manifold tends to pull away from the cylinder heads, thus allowing a small amount of water into the engine. Most of this water would evaporate when hot. This may be provoked by a hot spot at the back of the engine which may cause local overheating because of the way Reliant chose to pipe-up the SE6 heater.

Here is the evidence. First the heater was connected to the rear outlet, as used by Ford. This was to ensure that water circulated fully at the back of the cylinder block. Starting the engine from cold with thermocouples attached to the manifold next to the rear heater outlet (the outlet that has now reverted to its original purpose – bypass circulation), I found that the temperature rose at a steady rate of about 10 deg C per minute. The rear outlet heated up first and stayed about 4 deg C hotter all the way up. Returning from a run so the engine was thoroughly hot the heater outlet was 94 deg C and the bypass 90 deg C. When moving, the bypass temperature is about 85 deg C.

I suggest the reason for this is that, when the heater is connected to the proper outlet, water has passed through the engine from front to back and so gained more heat. It also means that water is circulating in the whole of the cylinder block, thus eliminating any dead spots where water does not circulate. Dead spots can be the cause of water loss. If water is circulating sluggishly around the area of the exhaust valves then local boiling can take place. This is most likely to occur under full power and may be an explanation for water loss when it is known for

KEEPING YOUR COOL

The new expansion tank mounts on top of the inlet manifold. The thermostat fits in its original position. Be careful when you take the old aluminium elbow off; the mounting bolts can be very rusty. Remember to use a pressure cap of the specific pressure.

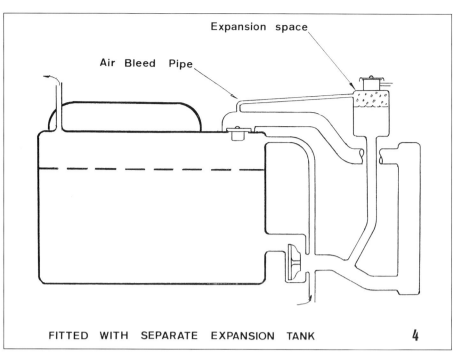

FITTED WITH SEPARATE EXPANSION TANK   4

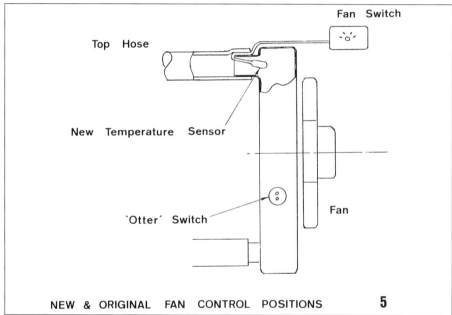

NEW & ORIGINAL FAN CONTROL POSITIONS   5

certain that a head gasket has not blown and there are no other obvious leaks.

Temperature troubles

As I worked on the car I became more interested and decided to find out how the cooling system functioned in practice. So the next experiment was to attach the thermocouple to the bottom of the water pump. This was quite revealing. Driving off on a cold winter's night (about 4 deg C) the temperature steadily rose up to 90 deg C. This took about 3 3/4 miles whereupon the thermostat opened and the temperature dropped to 50 deg C.

During this time the only water circulating in the engine was via the bypass and the heater outlet. Without the proper heater connection the only way for the water to circulate is through the small outlet by the thermostat housing. This bypass tube at the top is less than 3/8in diameter. It is evident that, without the proper heater connection, little water circulates in the engine until the thermostat opens. So although some may argue it is not essential to run the heater from the proper place, there are good technical and practical reasons to connect it up correctly.

Once the thermostat has opened, the bottom temperature cycles slowly between about 60 deg C and 70 deg C. Hard acceleration does not seem to change the temperature at the top of the engine perceptibly but, when accelerating hard in second, the temperature at the pump thermocouple rockets up to about 85 deg C by the time a gear change has to be made – yes, I do have the correct thermostat in with jiggle pin. This may be a route by which water could be lost.

In hotter weather, when the cooling system is working to capacity, hard acceleration may generate sufficient heat to boil the water, particularly if there is insufficient air circulating. Returning from the run the engine was left ticking over on the drive. It took only a few minutes for the water pump temperature to rise to 90 deg C when the fan cut in. It took ages for this to pull the temperature down to 85 deg C. The fan is clearly hardly adequate to cool the engine even in cold weather. More on this later.

Further thought suggested that, to complete the investigation, temperatures should

be taken on the bottom of the radiator. So on another cold night (ambient temperature 5 deg C) the radiator bottom temperature stayed, as expected, at 5 deg C until the thermostat opened at about the same mileage as before. Then it shot up 40 deg C and then cycled between 40 deg C and 60 deg C. It would rise to 80 deg C in short traffic queues. Moving the thermocouple to the top of the engine, actually taped to a distributor lead, gave information on underbonnet temperatures. Driving at about 50/60mph it ran about 20 deg C. Parked in the drive, leaving it until the fan cut in, registered 70 deg C.

Summer temperature estimates will be higher. To keep them in context, vehicle manufacturers for many years have specified an under-bonnet operating ambient temperature of 95 deg C. More recently, several years ago in fact, manufacturers started to request temperatures of up to 110 and 125 deg C. Against this is the major consideration that for many components every extra 10 deg C on the operating temperature doubles the failure rate.

Making comparisons between the size of

the fan on the Scimitar and other vehicles confirms that it is of inadequate size and poor efficiency. Many less powerful cars have better fans. However, fitting an effective fan will be a waste of time if it is not controlled properly. Examination of how the existing fan is controlled suggests that the position of the Otter switch is incorrect. The reason that the engine can overheat is that the Otter switch is set to about 80 deg C and it is fitted in the bottom half of the radiator. This means that the fan is not switched on until the engine is already close to overheating. The actual size of the radiator is more than adequate. The thermostatic switch should be fitted close to, or in, the top hose. I have fitted a Pacet Clover Fan and found it to be most satisfactory.

Overall the answer to the SE6 cooling problem is to provide sufficient pressurised expansion space for the hot water to go to, pipe up the heater as Ford intended, and fit an effective cooling fan with the thermostat switch in the correct position. The weather is hot now, I'm five months into the experiment and, so far, no coolant has been added.

A change for the better

As anyone who read our introductory story on Vinylkote will recall, this new product boasts a pretty impressive performance. However, our testing on that occasion was purely designed to illustrate, as graphically as possible, what it could do. In this case though we intend to put it through a much stiffer test by using it to re-colour a very faded and delapidated leather interior and a weather-beaten vinyl roof.

For those of you who missed our first article on this subject (February 1989) it might perhaps be useful to re-cap on what exactly Vinylkote is. To begin with the first important distinction to be made is that it is not a conventional covering like an upholstery paint but is, in fact, a chemically activated colouring compound which is absorbed into the surface to produce what the manufacturers claim to be a permanent change. Vinylkote represents a major breakthrough in re-colouring technology and the makers, Automotive and Industrial Chemicals Ltd, are convinced that it provides a totally credible alternative to the old, established paint-on colouring agents.

Their arguments do indeed appear to be strong. They maintain that two of the greatest problems associated with the established re-colouring products concern durability and the preservation of the original material texture. Because they work like a paint and, therefore, sit on the surface in a single layer, it is probable that with time they will crack, flake and fall off. In addition, the risk of obliterating the all-important grain pattern with this type of treatment is quite high unless great care is taken with the application.

Vinylkote, on the other hand, seems in practice to suffer from neither drawback because it is absorbed into the material, colouring as it goes, to settle in the sub-strata where it is completely protected from all potentially damaging influences. Consequently, the grain is left unaffected and the material remains just as supple and natural as it was before the treatment began.

Of course the proof of the pudding with this type of product lies in its lasting effect and, hopefully, the jobs undertaken in this feature will provide us with some long term answers to its usefulness.

We did the two jobs on separate occasions The second job undertaken was a re-colouring of the vinyl roof of my Scimitar. I had

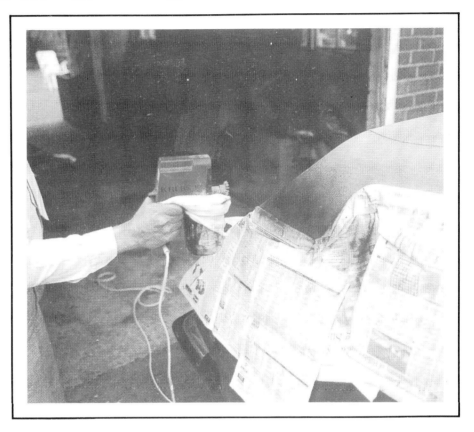

Putting Vinylkote to the test — Chris Graham reports

If you want a batch of mixed and matched Vinylkoye you must send a swatch for the factory to work from. For practical reasons it should be no smaller than this. The mixing service cost £4.

never been terribly happy with its original light tan finish and felt that, seeing as the bodywork is dark brown, it would look much better coloured black.

This job was much more straightforward as the pictures illustrate. The roof was thoroughly cleaned, masked and then sprayed with the same electric spray gun that Andrew had used for the XJ interior. The job was tackled out of doors and, although there was a slight breeze which did at times affect the performance of the gun, the job was finished within half-an-hour. The actual

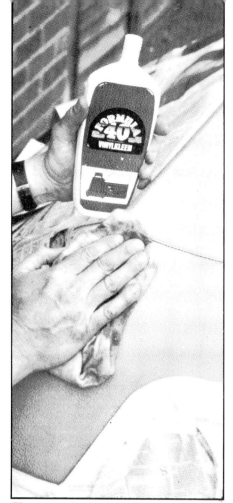

The preparation is vital when using Vinylkote. Every trace of silicone must be removed if the Vinylkote is to work successfully. The manufacturers recommend the use of Vinylkleen at this stage. Failure to clean properly will prevent absorbtion.

If you choose to buy your Vinylkote by the litre and apply it with a spray gun then thinners must be used to clean the gun. The KREBS electric spray gun shown here is ideal for applying Vinylkote from a litre can and is a very low cost tool for the job.

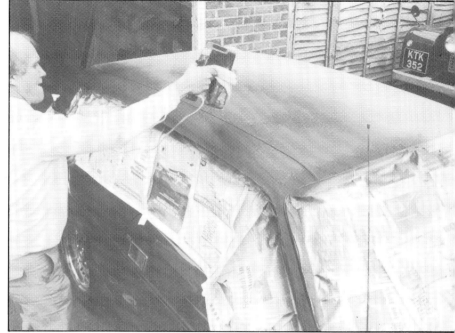

Masking is obviously important, especially when working outside where the spray is likely to be deflected by the wind. Andrew wrapped a cloth around the gun to guard against drips.

Within minutes of application the Vinylkote had worked its way in, leaving the grain perfectly distinct.

spraying time was only about 15 minutes but we applied two coats and allowed a 10-15 minute flash-off time in between. It took about half a litre of Vinylkote to re-colour the

If you happen to miss a spot, for whatever reason, then a small paint brush can be used to touch in the error.

Vinylsheen can be used to give the freshly treated material an attractive silky finish.

roof but you must remember that, because of the wind, this consumption is probably a little on the high side. The cost of this was £8.40.

In conclusion I must say that in both cases the quality of the finish achieved was excellent. Both look completely original and as good as new. You cannot tell that any change has been made. However, I shall be keeping a watchful eye on the condition of both jobs over the next six months to assess the all-important long-term durability of the finish.

Further information on Vinylkote and where it is available from can be obtained from Formula 40 (UK) Ltd, Kelsey House, High Street, Beckenham, Kent BR3 1AN. Tel: 081-663 3113.

ENGINE

Those with long memories may remember the stretched look of the Corsairs from Ford, with their four-cylinder 1.7- and 2-litre motors in V configuration a brand new look for the 1965 Motor Show. Then even bigger V lumps appeared in the Ford catalogue, with six cylinders and 3 litres capacity under the bonnets of Zephyrs and Zodiacs in the spring of 1966.

To overtake the Jones's, soon V6-powered Zephyrs, were superseded by the Consul and Granada series, again packing V6s of either 2.5 or 3 litres. Even more up-market Grannies used the faithful V6 in their time and were to do so until German Ford's 2.9 V6 took over.

Other V6 users

Apart from Ford themselves, Reliant were quick to swap the previous straight six, which the Tamworth minnow had first used in their Sabre Six, for Ford's newer, smoother running and more compact V6, fitting it in their sensationally Ogle-styled Scimitar GT from October 1966.

This 2994cc motor produced a then-mighty 128bhp at just 4750rpm. Lest we forget, Ford also produced a scaled-down 2495cc version from August 1967 for a while, with the same cylinder bore but different stroke. From August 1968, the GT's replacement Scimitar sports estate, the GTE, used the larger V6 too.

Even rarer, Welsh manufacturers Gilbern used both the 2.5- and 3-litre V6 for their Genie from 1966. Three years later, another handful of Gilbern's new Invaders mostly fell into British hands powered by a V6 apiece. In 1971, the Invader MkII and even rarer estate were also V6-equipped as was the MkIII in 1972. Trident were another long extinct marque to use Ford's trusty package for their Venturer in 1967.

Other Ford V6 original equipment users who survived those often financially hairy days of backyard manufacturing are TVR and Marcos, who chose the now famous engine with instant high power for their low weight glassfibre body providing them with a potent and practical package but at a realistic price.

TVR first used the V6 for the Tuscan in mid-'69 and, later, for their V6-powered M Series from 1972. While Jem Marsh, who surely produced and is still producing one of the most enduring Grand Touring shapes of all time, offered the V6 in his classic 3-litre Marcos and once did so, too, in the exceedingly rare Mantis four-seater.

Capris with grunt

Ford's 3-litre V6 appeared under a power-bulged bonnet in their own MkI Capri for the first time when the 3000GT hit the streets in October 1969. Reliant and Ford's other OE customers benefited from a bhp increase two years later.

Capri MkII, S and Series 3 models could all be chosen with the V6 but perhaps the wildest Ford car application of them all was when the Competi-

Richard Hudson-Evans reports on rebuilding the widely encountered Ford V6 3-litre.

To remove a V6 from a Scimitar, for example, takes Will Sparrow's team about three hours. Allow up to one-and-a-half hours to take the motor out of a Capri or Granada as accessibility is better.

Although it is a very sound engine, a change of fibre gear and oil pump drive is a wise precaution after 70,000-75,000 miles. A V6 should then be good for 150,000 miles before a major overhaul is necessary. One recent unit from a GTE had covered 175,000 miles without ever being touched.

Once it is out of a car, stripping down the motor should take only two hours. Cleaning up all the components can take two days though, as these engines do tend to sludge up inside and out.

Removing the old core plugs is vital as this block can silt up internally in its waterways. The levels of sludge can rise, preventing the proper circulation of water and hampering cooling. Although the core plugs may look sound on the outside, they're almost certain to be worn out on the inside with corrosion and just about to leak. So change them, says Will.

With core plugs removed, this V6 block has been reconditioned. It has been rebored and the gasket faces on the top of the block for both heads have been refaced. This is advisable apparently to prevent subsequent head gasket problems.

Fresh back from machining, ideally a block should be pressure-washed with a steam cleaner and then have all its oilways blown through with an airline to ensure that it's really clean before assembly.

A nice shiny set of V6 bores. Note the slight chamfer cut-out round the top of the bore holes preferred by Will. If you just had a squared-off edge it can be all too easy to trap a ring when sliding the piston assemblies from the piston clamp into the bores.

New pistons, fitted to original rods, to match the bores have been used here. Each gudgeon pin is a press-fit into its con-rod – heat is usually needed to make life easier when fitting them.

Before building up a V6, it's important to turn each piston and rod upside down to oil the gudgeon pin really well, working it to and fro so that there's plenty of oil up inside each piston in readiness for start-up. Don't merely rely on the lubrication of the oil splash of initial start-up for a newly rebuilt motor, warns Will. And, as with any engine rebuild, of course, it pays to lay everything out neatly and cleanly while you work.

Before re-employing a camshaft, inspect it very carefully for wear on the lobes. Wear on either side of the main tip of the lobe is common on the V6. You can usually detect this by spotting imperfections in the metal next to a slightly polished area on the lobe tips. If this is the case the cam should be scrapped or exchanged for a reprofiled unit – maybe using a Stage One cam instead, thus gaining a few more bhp at the same time.

When the crankshaft's main and big-end journals have been reground, which is fairly commonly needed, there may well be fine metal particles from the crank in the oilways as well as bits off the grinding wheel. Again, use a steam cleaner and pressure washer to clear each individual oilway hole very carefully. Quickly clean all traces of water from head and oilways with an airline to prevent any corrosion. A crank can be ground down by 40thou, so should take up to four regrinds before a replacement is a better bet.

tions Department at Boreham employed the V6 to power their pioneering – and years ahead of its time remember – four-wheel-drive Capris for TV Rallycross.

The V6 constitution

The V6 has six cylinders arranged in two banks of three pots aside, inclined at 60 degrees to each other and offset. The bores are machined directly into the blocks which are integral with the crank-case, the bottom of which is enclosed by a steel sump pan. Cast iron cylinder liners may be fitted.

The crank has four main bearings with renew-able shells. End float is controlled by thrust wash-ers at the front intermediate housing and oil seals are fitted to both front cover and rear seal carrier. Conrod big-ends have renewable bearing shells. Small-ends are shrunk-fit to the gudgeon pins.

The combustion chambers are machined into the crowns of the pistons which are fitted with a pair of compression rings and one oil control ring. Gudgeon pin bores are offset in each piston towards the thrust side to counterbalance gas load during firing stroke.

Both distributor and oil pump, either twin rotor or vane type, are driven by a skew gear which is part of the camshaft, an eccentric on the cam also operating the fuel pump.

A single inlet manifold carries the single twin-choke carburettor, a Weber 40 DFA/1 or 38 DGAS/3A. The later carb is supposed to be tam-per-proof with plugs sealing off screws, thus elim-inating all adjustments bar idling speed. The choke is automatic, operating thermostatically according to the coolant's temperature. The later

V6 cylinder heads should always be skimmed as they invariably warp. During the build-up of each head, note an oil can being used here to lubricate those valve guides and stems.

Lap in the valves carefully too. Will always has his V6 heads' valve seats and head faces refaced, enabling speedy grinding-in with a fine paste and therefore achieving a perfect seal afterwards.

Here's a fully built up V6 head ready for popping on to one bank of the block. As required, valves have been cleaned up or replaced and new seat inserts fitted. Oilways and waterways have been blown out before new core plugs have been fitted.

If this engine is run short of water, perhaps after a hose has leaked or blown, or maybe after the thermostat has stuck, one or both of a V6's head gaskets are prone to becoming damaged. This is where a V6 head will usually blow. Across the face next to the centre waterway is where the head may have warped up.

A new oil pump is about to be fitted. At around £30 for a new one, it's false economy not to replace this during a major rebuild. The oil pick-up pipe can become gunged up internally too, so Will pops his into a caustic bath before refitting to clear out any internal sludge and, of course, it will have been blown dry with an airline too.

It normally takes a V6 regular, like Will, a full working day to build up a V6 because many things should be checked throughout asssembly.

Starting with the crank going into the block, make sure that all bearing caps are straight and true. The crank should spin quite freely when it's fitted. As each piston goes in, the crank should be turned over again to ensure that each piston has the same amount of resistance.

An amateur using the manual should allow a couple of days to avoid mistakes.

Inlet manifolds should be bead-blasted to clean them out thoroughly and to give them a good finish. Again, it's important to ensure that any sludge has been removed from inlet manifold waterways. Before refitting an inlet manifold on a motor, dunk well in a degreaser.

Always fit a new fibre gear too. These really must be regarded as a throw-away item. You can never tell when one is going to fail. So fit a new one as a matter of course.

taking your Scimitar, let us say, into a specialist like Will and driving out two days later with a properly fitted exchange engine, budget for between £1000 and £1200.

For supplying an exchange engine, with you doing the removal and installation work yourself, this firm would charge you about £500. But we're not talking about paying for any old re-con motor with perhaps little more than a new set of gaskets and a coat of paint!

V6 souping

The quickest and most cost-effective way to improve the performance on the V6 is by changing the cam, which could be worth 15-20bhp. It's also important to 'de-fuzz' the inlet manifold internal airways and clean up the head porting too, being careful to match them up exactly.

The standard Weber is a twin-choke unit with both chokes operating together and is reckoned to be pretty good unless you want to spend a lot of money on a triple Weber or a single Holley installation.

Much more worthwhile, in terms of £p spent for bhp gained, would be fitting a decent three-branch exhaust system. Fitting bigger valves to the heads is helpful too. However, the standard motor is good for 134bhp which I would suggest will be sufficient for most legal purposes.

My thanks for much advice in the preparation of this feature is Will Sparrow Ltd, Bidavon Industrial Estate, Bidford-upon-Avon, Warwickshire (Tel: 0789 490441).

Putting a rebuilt V6 back into the car will often be the most time-consuming job of all. There are always so many extra jobs to do that you won't have budgeted for ... hoses will need sorting out...ends of pipes will have to be cleaned up ... wiring may need to be tidied up.

air filter incorporates a thermostatically controlled and servo-operated flap valve.

When a manual box is fitted, the clutch operates directly on to the flywheel's rear face, being provided with a ring gear for starter motor pinion engagement. For auto transmissions, of course, the traditional flywheel will have been replaced by a torque converter drive plate.

Having it done

If you don't want to get stuck in yourself and prefer having a transplant carried out by experts,